INCREDIBLE
FACTS FOR INQUISITIVE MINDS

Mind-Boggling Facts About Science, History,
Pop Culture & The Weird World We Live in

FRED FLYNN

INCREDIBLE FACTS FOR INQUISITIVE MINDS

Mind-Boggling Facts About Science, History, Pop Culture & The Weird World We Live in

ISBN: 978-1-922590-59-6

TABLE OF CONTENTS

INTRODUCTION

GREETINGS, ADVENTUROUS TRIVIA HUNTERS
and fact-loving friends! If you're holding this book,
it means you're just like us - perpetually curious, constantly
questioning, and never satisfied with the mundane.
It's clear that you're a breed apart - the kind of person
who thrills in the discovery of the weird, the wonderful,
and the downright bonkers facts about the fabric of our
shared universe.

You might have pondered why your skin pricks up into
goosebumps when you hear your favorite song, the reason
cats love to purr when stroked, or where the high-five
originated... these are but mere scratches on the surface
of the vast ocean of knowledge that awaits you in
"incredible Facts for inquisitive Minds".

This trivia treasure trove is neatly segmented into easily
navigable chapters, each crammed with hundreds of
astounding facts that are sure to blow your mind. Read it
sequentially, hop around to chapters that tickle your fancy,
or even read it upside down if that's your jam!

Get ready for the ride of your life as we embark on
this whirlwind journey through the most intriguing and
occasionally downright bizarre facts known to humankind!

SO BUCKLE UP, FACTONAUTS;

YOUR ADVENTURE BEGINS NOW!

CHAPTER ONE

SPECTACULAR SCIENCE & TECH TRIUMPHS

INVENTIONS YOU NEVER KNEW EXISTED

> **CAN YOU BELIEVE THAT BEFORE THE ELECTRIC**
fan, there was the "human-powered fan"? The Punkah,
invented in ancient india, was a large swinging fan operated
by a servant pulling a rope. Talk about a labor-intensive
way to stay cool!

> **THOMAS EDISON MAY BE FAMOUS FOR**
inventing the light bulb, but did you know he also tried to
create a "spirit phone" to communicate with the dead?
This endeavor was partly motivated by his rivalry with
Nikola Tesla, another giant in the field of electrical
engineering and invention, who had also expressed interest
in the possibility of using technology to interact with
the supernatural. Sadly, no one ever managed to dial up
a ghost with his eerie invention.

> **CAN YOU IMAGINE**
a "flying car"? in 1946,
visionary engineer Robert
Edison Fulton, Jr. dared
to dream and invented the
"Airphibian". It could fly to
an airport and then, after
disengaging wings, tail, and
propeller, become a car. Though
it never soared in the commercial
market, it certainly had our
heads in the clouds!

> **INTRODUCING THE "BABY CAGE"!** DREAMT UP in the bustling 1920s, this daring invention enabled metropolitan moms and dads to attach a wire mesh cage, akin to a tiny terrace playpen, and hang it precariously from their windows. The result? Their mini munchkins could get some refreshing air with a cityscape view. London, England, was the epicenter of this high-flying fad, as parents took child-rearing to new extremes—quite literally!

> **PICTURE THIS:** THE "RAINY day cigarette holder" from the 1920s, a tiny umbrella for your cigarette. This dainty accessory promised to keep your smoke dry no matter the downpour, because heaven forbid your cigarette gets a soaking before you do.

> **SAY HELLO TO THE "BABY mop"!** in 1998, this peculiar product turned crawling babies into little cleaning machines. The onesie, fitted with mop-like fabric, allowed babies to clean floors as they explored their surroundings, proving that even infants can multitask!

> **DID YOU KNOW THAT NIKOLA TESLA,** the wizard of electrical invention, dreamt up an "earthquake machine"? Tesla's mechanical oscillator, developed in the late 19th century, could allegedly generate seismic shocks powerful enough to shake buildings to their core. While he claimed to have tested it successfully, the fear of actually triggering an earthquake led him to dismantle the device. Perhaps it's for the best; we're not quite ready for DIY tectonics.

> **THE AMPHIBIOUS BICYCLE, A PARISIAN** invention from 1932, promised to take you from land to lake without missing a pedal. Carrying a load of 120 pounds, this bike was the swiss army knife of transportation, enabling you to not walk, but "cycle" on water. Unfortunately, it seems most cyclists preferred to keep their wheels and water separate.

> **ENTER THE "ISOLATOR," A 1925 INVENTION** designed to eliminate workplace distractions before the age of smartphones. This helmet enclosed the wearer's head, limiting vision and hearing, supposedly enhancing focus. It even piped in oxygen! Perfect for those who find today's open-plan offices a bit too communal, though it might make coffee breaks a tad challenging.

> **IN THE 1960s, AN UNLIKELY COSMETIC ITEM** was coverted into a lethal weapon. Designed for KGB operatives, it disguised a single-shot firearm as a innocent tube of lipstick. a lethal blend of fashion and espionage!

> **DIVE INTO THE QUIRKY** world of "anti-bandit bags" developed in the 1960s. These handbags were designed for women to protect their valuables. If a thief tried to snatch the bag, it would automatically release a dye, staining the robber (and potentially the contents of the bag) in a vivid hue. Talk about catching a thief red-handed!

> IN THE **1930s**, NIKOLA TESLA CONJURED UP
the "Teleforce," better known as the "Death Ray." This
formidable invention was designed to shoot particle beams
capable of bringing down enemy aircraft and armies from
afar. Tesla envisioned this as a weapon to end all wars.
However, despite its awe-inspiring premise, the Death Ray
was never tested publicly, and Tesla kept the technical
details a closely guarded secret. Thus, the Death Ray
straddles the line between groundbreaking scientific
invention and the realms of science fiction.

> EVER WANTED TO COMPLETELY ESCAPE THE
world and take a nap anywhere? Enter the Ostrich Pillow,
a pillow you wear like a helmet, with holes for your mouth
and nose. It's perfect for napping in public without the
awkward eye contact.

> DID YOU KNOW THE BEACH SCENE OF THE
1920s had its own tech twist with "wooden bathing suits"?
invented in Hoquiam, Washington, in 1929, these buoyant
suits were designed to make swimming "easier". Imagine
floating around, literally stiff as a board, while trying to
catch some waves. It seems fashion and flotation devices
had a brief, rather plank-like, romance.

ECCENTRIC QUIRKS OF
BRILLIANT MINDS

> DID YOU KNOW THAT LEGENDARY PHYSICIST,
Richard Feynman, was a compulsive bongo player! When
he wasn't unraveling the mysteries of quantum mechanics,
he was pounding out rhythms on his beloved drums.

> **DID YOU KNOW THAT SIR ISAAC NEWTON,** the man who discovered gravity, had a penchant for alchemy? That's right! He spent years trying to turn base metals into gold. Talk about a heavy obsession!

> **NIKOLA TESLA WAS OBSESSED WITH THE** number three. Tesla would also often walk around a block three times before entering a building and would use 18 napkins to clean his plates, which is six times three. When it came to hotel rooms, he preferred staying in rooms with numbers divisible by three. He also had work hours planned around these numbers, working from 9 a.m. to 6 p.m., and even his dining schedule aligned with this numerical pattern, opting to dine precisely at 8:10 p.m., because when you add the digits 8 and 10, you get 18, again divisible by three We wonder if these shocking habits electrified his genius!

> **WHO KNEW THE FATHER OF MODERN PHYSICS,** Albert Einstein, was a passionate violinist? He once said that if he hadn't been a scientist, he would have been a musician. From $E=mc^2$ to a sweet symphony!

> **ALBERT ALSO DECLARED A LIFELONG FEUD** against... socks? It turns out, Einstein's disdain for these foot-huggers wasn't a fashion statement but a rebellion against the tyranny of holes. As a child, he found sock holes so distracting, he decided his thoughts were too precious to waste on such trivial matters.

> **AND THEN THERE'S THE CASE OF EINSTEIN'S** love affair with his pillow, dedicating a whopping 10 hours a day to the art of slumber. In a world where sleep is often sacrificed at the altar of productivity, Einstein snoozed defiantly. This wasn't laziness; it was his brain

demanding the rest it deserved for solving the mysteries of the universe. So, if anyone ever calls you a sleepyhead, just remember, you're in Nobel company!

> ### DURING NAPS, EINSTEIN USED A SPOON
as a makeshift alarm clock. Holding a spoon over a metal plate, he'd nap until he dropped the spoon against the plate, waking him up. This ingenious method kept his naps short, ensuring his brain remained primed for breakthrough ideas.

> ### STEVE JOBS, THE VISIONARY BEHIND APPLE,
had a fruitarian phase, believing a diet of primarily fruits would eliminate the need for showers. Spoiler alert: it didn't. But it did lead to naming his company 'Apple', marking a blend of dietary preferences with technological innovation.

> ### MARK TWAIN, THE FATHER OF AMERICAN
literature, was known for his love of white suits. He wore them exclusively in his later years, regardless of the season, making him a *white-hot* literary figure.

> ### LUDWIG VAN BEETHOVEN,
the maestro of symphonies, had a meticulous ritual for his coffee. He insisted on using exactly 60 beans per cup, counting them out one by one. Perhaps this precision was the secret ingredient to his timeless compositions.

> **SALVADOR DALÍ'S ECCENTRICITY**
wasn't limited to his art; it extended into
his choice of pets as well. Believe it or not,
he once took an anteater for a walk in the
streets of Paris. With a leash around
its neck, the anteater
accompanied Dalí,
turning heads and
probably hoovering
up any ants in sight.

> **THE PHYSICIST MARIE CURIE, FAMOUS FOR**
her groundbreaking work on radioactivity, had a strange
habit of carrying test tubes filled with radioactive
substances in her pockets, unaware of the dangers they
posed. We can only imagine the glowing conversations she
must have had!

> **THOMAS EDISON, THE PROLIFIC INVENTOR**
behind the light bulb, had a peculiar way of interviewing
potential employees. He'd serve them soup and if they
salted it before tasting, they wouldn't get the job. Edison
believed it showed a lack of analysis before action, a key
ingredient for innovation that's a bit hard to digest.

> **LEONARDO DA VINCI, THE QUINTESSENTIAL**
Renaissance man, wrote most of his notes in mirror writing.
He'd write from right to left, making it a reflective task
to decipher his genius. Whether it was for secrecy or just
because he could, it adds an extra layer of mystery to his
already fascinating work.

> **HOWARD HUGHES, THE BILLIONAIRE AVIATOR,**
filmmaker, and inventor, had obsessive-compulsive
disorder, which manifested in peculiar ways. Among his

many quirks, he had a fixation on the size of peas and used a special screening device to sort them by size before eating. It seems even his vegetables had to be up to standards.

> MICHAEL FARADAY, KNOWN FOR HIS discoveries in electromagnetism, had a less scientific ritual of always turning his teacup so the handle faced a specific direction. Perhaps in his mind, it was a small way to ensure the forces of the universe remained aligned – or maybe he just liked knowing where to grab his tea.

> CHARLES DICKENS, THE ILLUSTRIOUS AUTHOR of classics such as "A Christmas Carol," had a peculiar nighttime ritual to ensure a good night's sleep. He insisted on sleeping aligned with the cardinal points, with his bed facing north-south, believing it improved his creativity and inspiration. Perhaps his literary genius was magnetically charged!

> THE LEGENDARY ASTROPHYSICIST STEPHEN Hawking loved zero-gravity flights! He once experienced weightlessness during a parabolic flight, soaring through the sky like a superhuman. Who said science can't be thrilling?

ACCIDENTAL INVENTIONS

> CAN YOU BELIEVE THAT SUPER GLUE WAS initially a mistake? It's true! Dr. Harry Coover accidentally discovered the powerful adhesive during WWII when he was searching for materials to make clear plastic

gun sights. Instead, he stumbled upon cyanoacrylate, a stubborn adhesive that bonded things together at lightning speed – and now it's a staple in every household!

> **WOULD YOU GUESS THAT THE MICROWAVE** oven has its origins in radar technology? Percy Spencer, a self-taught engineer, was working with radar equipment when he noticed that the chocolate bar in his pocket had melted. Intrigued, he tested popcorn and eggs next, leading to the development of the first microwave oven, an appliance that has revolutionized cooking across the globe!

> **YOU WON'T BELIEVE HOW THE SLINKY TOY** came to be! in 1943, naval engineer Richard James was working on a project to develop springs for stabilizing sensitive shipboard instruments when he accidentally knocked a spring off the shelf. As it gracefully "walked" down a stack of books, he realized he had created an iconic toy that would captivate millions of children for generations!

> **DID YOU KNOW THE STORY** behind the invention of the pacemaker? Believe it or not, it started with a simple mistake. In 1956, Wilson Greatbatch was working on a heart rhythm recording device when he accidentally inserted the wrong resistor. To his astonishment, the circuit produced electrical pulses similar to a heartbeat, leading to the life-saving invention that has since benefited millions of people worldwide!

> **CAN YOU IMAGINE A WORLD WITHOUT**
Velcro? Swiss engineer George de Mestral might've never invented it if he hadn't gone for a walk with his dog! After a hike in 1941, George noticed that burrs from plants were sticking to his clothes and his dog's fur. Intrigued, he examined the burrs under a microscope and discovered their hook-like structure, inspiring him to create the revolutionary fastener we know today!

> **WHO WOULD'VE THOUGHT THAT AN ICE-COLD**
drink could lead to the invention of air conditioning? in 1902, Willis Carrier was working at a publishing company to solve a humidity problem affecting the printing process. He designed a machine that could control humidity using chilled water coils, and voila – the world's first modern air conditioner was born, forever changing how we handle hot summer days!

> **DID YOU KNOW THAT THE DISCOVERY OF X-RAYS**
was a happy accident? in 1895, German physicist Wilhelm Conrad Röntgen was experimenting with cathode rays when he noticed that a fluorescent screen in his lab started to glow. Curious, Röntgen placed various objects between the screen and the cathode ray tube, eventually discovering that he could see the bones in his hand! This groundbreaking discovery led to the development of X-ray technology, forever changing the fields of medicine and science.

> **DID YOU KNOW THAT THE INVENTOR OF**
the traffic light got his idea from a child's toy? in 1912, Lester Wire, a Salt Lake City police officer, was inspired by a birdhouse-like toy with doors that opened and closed to reveal the words "stop" and "go." Wire's invention became the first electric traffic light, significantly improving traffic safety and forever changing the way we navigate our roads!

> **CAN YOU IMAGINE A WORLD FREE OF PLASTIC?**
It's a twist of fate that in 1907, Belgian chemist Leo
Baekeland stumbled upon Bakelite, the first synthetic plastic,
while trying to whip up a synthetic alternative to shellac (you
know, that fancy insect-produced resin). Little did he know,
his moldable, heat-resistant creation would spark a plastic
obsession, leaving us drowning in a sea of pollution. Now,
our planet's critters and ecosystems are paying the price,
making us question whether this serendipitous invention was
a blessing or a curse in disguise!

> **CAN YOU IMAGINE HOW A BROKEN JAR LED**
to the invention of tempered glass? in 1908, French
scientist Edouard Bénédictus dropped a glass jar
containing a film of cellulose nitrate. The jar cracked but
didn't shatter into dangerous shards. This serendipitous
discovery led to the development of safety glass, which
is now used in car windows, glass doors, and smartphones,
providing an extra layer of protection in our daily lives!

> **CAN YOU BELIEVE THAT THE IDEA FOR**
eyeglasses came from monks using handheld magnifying
glasses? in the 13th century, monks would use glass
spheres filled with water or polished glass to magnify
texts, making it easier to read. Eventually, someone came
up with the idea of mounting these lenses on a frame,
creating the first pair of eyeglasses. Today, eyeglasses are
an essential part of many people's lives, improving vision
and making daily tasks much more manageable!

> **READY FOR A CAFFEINE JOLT OF TRIVIA?**
It's hard to believe that the invention of instant
coffee was a total fluke! in 1901, Japanese-American
chemist Satori Kato was all about preserving coffee via
freeze-drying when he unexpectedly whipped up the first

batch of instant coffee. Now, this marvel of convenience keeps us perky on-the-go and has become an integral part of countless hurried mornings and late-night cram sessions. Thanks for the quick fix, Mr. Kato!

> **DID YOU KNOW THAT THE ORIGINAL PURPOSE** of bubble wrap was far from packing material? in 1957, inventors Alfred Fielding and Marc Chavannes were attempting to create textured wallpaper by sealing two shower curtains together. Although their wallpaper idea flopped, they discovered that their creation made an excellent protective cushioning for fragile items. Today, bubble wrap not only safeguards our precious belongings during shipping but also provides us with endless popping satisfaction!

> **CAN YOU BELIEVE THAT THE CREATION OF** Silly Putty stemmed from a World War II rubber shortage? in 1943, engineer James Wright was trying to invent a synthetic rubber substitute for General Electric. Instead of creating the rubber he was aiming for, he stumbled upon a bouncy, stretchy substance that became Silly Putty. This quirky, moldable material has since become a classic childhood toy, providing hours of entertainment for kids and adults alike!

HISTORIES
TECH MISHAPS

> **IT'S TIME TO DELVE INTO THE COMICALLY** catastrophic world of historical tech mishaps! Remember the Hubble Space Telescope? Launched in 1990, this

sophisticated piece of space tech was designed to snap crystal-clear images of the cosmos. Alas, a tiny miscalculation in the telescope's mirror resulted in embarrassingly blurry photos, earning Hubble the nickname "Hubble's Bubble." Thankfully, after a costly repair mission, the telescope went on to capture some of the most stunning images of our universe!

> ### PICTURE THIS: IT's 1858, AND LONDON

is hit with the "Great Stink." Sounds dreadful, right? Well, that's because it was! The city's outdated sewer system couldn't handle the population boom, leading to a stench so unbearable it disrupted Parliament's work. This smelly disaster prompted a massive overhaul of London's sanitation infrastructure, transforming it into a modern marvel of engineering. So, the next time you take a whiff of fresh air, spare a thought for those who endured the Great Stink!

> ### REMEMBER THE HINDENBURG DISASTER?

in 1937, this luxurious airship was the epitome of cutting-edge aviation technology. But during a fateful docking in New Jersey, the hydrogen-filled Hindenburg suddenly burst into flames, tragically killing

36 people. This catastrophic event marked the end of the airship era and reinforced the notion that hydrogen and air travel don't mix! a poignant reminder that even the loftiest of human achievements can come crashing down in a fiery blaze.

> **Ever heard of the Vasa? This Swedish** warship was supposed to be the pride of the navy when it set sail in 1628. But due to a poorly designed hull, the top-heavy vessel capsized and sank just minutes into its maiden voyage! The Vasa's disastrous plunge became a humiliating lesson in the importance of ship stability, proving that even the most imposing vessels can't defy the laws of physics. Sailing away with a sinking feeling, anyone?

> **Ever heard of the "Mars Climate** Orbiter"? Launched in 1998, this NASA spacecraft was on a mission to study the Red Planet's atmosphere. But due to a colossal mix-up between metric and imperial units, the $125 million orbiter went off course and was destroyed upon entering Mars' atmosphere. This astronomical blunder taught us that sometimes, even rocket scientists can get their measurements wrong!

> **Have you ever heard** of the "Millennium Bug"? As the world prepared to usher in the year 2000, panic ensued over a potential global catastrophe caused by a tiny computer glitch. Many computer systems used only two digits to represent the year, causing fears that the rollover from '99 to '00 would lead to widespread chaos. Billions of

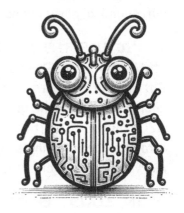

dollars were spent to fix the problem, yet when the clock struck midnight, the dreaded Y2K bug was little more than a whimper. a true testament to the power of paranoia and the cost of short-sighted programming!

> **HAVE YOU EVER WONDERED HOW A SINGLE** typo could cost millions of dollars? in 2012, the financial world gasped in disbelief as a rogue algorithm from the trading firm Knight Capital went haywire, causing massive market disruptions. This costly coding error led to a staggering $440 million loss in just 45 minutes, ultimately forcing the company to be acquired by another firm. a jaw-dropping reminder that in the digital age, even a tiny mistake can have colossal consequences!

> **LET'S VENTURE BACK TO 1962 AND THE** disastrous launch of NASA's Mariner 1 spacecraft. Intended to explore Venus, the probe veered off course shortly after lift-off due to a single omitted hyphen in its guidance system's code. The result? a $150 million explosion, as the spacecraft had to be destroyed to prevent a potential crash back to Earth. a costly reminder that even the tiniest details can have astronomical consequences!

> **PICTURE THE SCENE: A BRAND-NEW,** state-of-the-art Russian satellite, all set for launch. But alas, in 2013, a technician entered the wrong coordinates into the guidance system, causing the $200 million satellite to veer off course and plummet into the ocean. a single typo turned this high-tech marvel into a watery wreck – now that's a costly mistake!

> **IN 2009, GOOGLE'S ATTEMPT TO UPDATE** its search engine turned into a digital disaster. a human error caused Google to mistakenly flag the entire internet as malware, leaving millions of users flabbergasted and unable to access their favorite websites. The glitch was fixed in a matter of hours, but it left the tech giant red-faced and users questioning their online security.

> **YOU'VE HEARD OF "TOO BIG TO FAIL,"** but how about "too big to sail"? in 2014, a colossal container ship named the Ever Given got stuck in the Suez Canal, blocking one of the world's busiest trade routes for six excruciating days. The mishap cost an estimated $59 billion in global trade losses, all because of a minor navigational error. It just goes to show that even the best-laid plans can go awry – and sometimes, size does matter!

INVENTORS & THEIR BRILLIANT BREAKTHROUGHS

> **CAN YOU IMAGINE A WORLD WITHOUT THE** telephone? Well, thanks to Alexander Graham Bell, we don't have to! He made the first successful telephone call in 1876, whispering the famous words, "Mr. Watson, come here; I want to see you." This miraculous invention shrunk the world, connecting people miles apart like never before.

> **PICTURE THIS: YOU'RE** chilling in your living room when suddenly you realize you can't see a thing! Enter Thomas Edison, the man behind the lightbulb. Though not the sole inventor, Edison's 1879 creation outshone others, lasting 1,200 hours! That's like 50 days of non-stop brightness, folks!

> **ARE YOU A FAN OF TAKING SELFIES? YOU CAN** thank the "Father of Photography," Louis Daguerre! in 1839, he developed the daguerreotype, an early photograph with crisp detail. Back then, you had to sit still for 15 minutes to get a perfect shot, but hey, no more blurry selfies!

> **EVER WONDERED HOW PEOPLE DISCOVERED GERMS** before microscopes? Well, they didn't! It wasn't until 1674 when Antonie van Leeuwenhoek peered through his homemade microscope and discovered a microscopic world. Imagine all those unseen critters, just waiting to be found!

> **BORED OF WALKING? MEET KARL BENZ,** the man who put the world on wheels! in 1885, he created the first gasoline-powered automobile, the Benz Patent-Motorwagen. It traveled at a whopping 10 mph, which might not impress today's speed demons, but it sure did rev up the future of transportation!

> **LOVE THE SMELL OF FRESHLY PRINTED BOOKS?** Johannes Gutenberg's your man! in 1440, he introduced the movable type printing press, making mass production of books possible. Suddenly, knowledge was available to the masses, spreading faster than you can say "Biblio-mania!"

> **CAN YOU BELIEVE** people used to send messages by horse? Thank goodness for Samuel Morse and his telegraph! in 1844, he sent the first telegraph message, "What hath God wrought!" and forever changed communication. So long, Pony Express!

INCREDIBLE FACTS FOR INQUISITIVE MINDS

> EVER GET LOST WITHOUT YOUR GPS?

You can thank Roger Easton for finding your way! in 1978, he launched the first Global Positioning System (GPS) satellite, changing navigation forever. Now we can find the nearest pizza place in a snap!

> EVER WONDERED HOW YOU'D SURVIVE

without your morning latte? Thank Keurig for making coffee easier! in 1998, they introduced their single-cup brewing system, giving coffee lovers the perfect cup in record time.

> FASTER THAN A SPEEDING BULLET – IT'S THE

Large Hadron Collider! This gargantuan particle accelerator, completed in 2008, smashes subatomic particles together at a whopping 99.9999991% the speed of light. To put that into perspective, it's like traveling around the Earth over seven times in just one second! The LHC has unlocked new frontiers in physics, including the discovery of the elusive Higgs boson. But beware! Some critics have raised concerns about potential dangers, such as the creation of microscopic black holes. Nevertheless, the benefits of understanding the fundamental forces of our universe are truly astounding.

> RAIN, RAIN, COME OUR WAY! DID YOU

know we can actually create rain using a fascinating technology called cloud seeding? Developed in the 1940s by American chemist Vincent Schaefer, cloud seeding involves dispersing substances like silver iodide or dry ice into the atmosphere to stimulate precipitation. This weather-modifying wizardry can help combat drought, increase water supply, and even control hailstorms. Talk about a silver (iodide) lining in the clouds! So next time you're doing a rain dance, remember that science has got you covered too!

> ## THE AMAZING TECHNOLOGY OF DESALINATION
swoops in to save our parched planet! Dating back to the 1960s, desalination was first commercialized by Sidney Loeb, an American engineer who pioneered the reverse osmosis technique. This salt-busting superhero of a process removes salt and other impurities from seawater, transforming it into drinkable H_2O. With around 71% of our planet's surface draped in water, it's time to wave goodbye to the idea of running out of water. Here's to a future where thirst is a thing of the past!

> ## CAN YOU PICTURE LIFE BEFORE REFRIGERATORS?
Ice boxes were all the rage until Fred W. Wolf Jr. froze the competition with the invention of the first electric refrigerator in 1913. This cool contraption changed kitchens forever, making it a breeze to keep food fresh. Say goodbye to daily trips to the market and hello to ice cream at midnight!

> ## BEFORE THE ERA OF
digital wonders, the world spun vinyl. Emile Berliner revolutionized music with his invention of the gramophone and flat disc records in 1887. This spin-tastic device brought music into homes, making Berliner the unsung hero of dance parties and heartbreak solos. From classical to rock, the gramophone had it covered.

INCREDIBLE FACTS FOR INQUISITIVE MINDS

> **HAVE YOU EVER MARVELED AT SKYSCRAPERS** and wondered how they were built so tall? Enter Elisha Otis, the father of the modern elevator, who in 1852 made high-rise buildings practical. His safety elevator prevented the car from falling if the lifting rope broke, elevating our cityscapes quite literally. Thanks to Otis, the sky's the limit!

> **EVER PONDERED HOW PEOPLE KEPT TIME** before wristwatches? Patek Philippe & Co. crafted the first wristwatch in 1868, transforming how we manage our time. This tick-tock trendsetter wrapped the concept of punctuality around our wrists, making timekeeping both a fashion statement and a functional necessity.

> **NIKOLA TESLA'S** dream of wireless communication became a reality with his work on the Tesla coil in the 1890s. Though Marconi is often credited with the invention of the radio, Tesla's contributions laid the groundwork for wireless technologies that connect us today.

> **THE HUMBLE WASHING MACHINE HAS** scrubbed its way into our lives, thanks to James King who patented the first hand-powered machine in 1851. This revolutionary invention wrung out the old ways of labor-intensive laundry, making clean clothes a less draining task. King's creation paved the way for modern machines that spin our clothes to perfection.

> **KNOWN AS THE "BLACK EDISON," GRANVILLE** T. Woods electrified the world with over 50 patents, improving electric railway systems and communication lines. His most famous invention, the Synchronous Multiplex Railway Telegraph in 1887, made train travel safer by enabling communication between stations. Thanks to Woods, the 'railway telegraphy' system kept countless trains from colliding.

> **IN 1986, AN OPHTHALMOLOGIST NAMED** Patricia Bath patented the Laserphaco Probe, revolutionizing cataract surgery. Her invention restored sight to those who'd been blind for over 30 years! Bath wasn't just clearing up vision; she was also a visionary in medical technology and breaking through the hazy barriers for women of color in science.

> **ON A CHILLY NIGHT IN 1919, ALICE H.** Parker devised a system of gas-powered central heating that brought warmth to homes like never before. Her design eliminated the need for wood-burning stoves, giving rise to the modern thermostat-controlled heating systems. Thanks to Alice, staying toasty doesn't mean stoking the fire all night!

THE WORLD CRAZIEST
MAN MADE STRUCTURES

> **CAN YOU FATHOM THE SHEER SIZE OF THE** Great Wall of China? This colossal construction, built between the 7th century BC and the 17th century AD, stretches over 13,170 miles (21,196 kilometers), making

INCREDIBLE FACTS FOR INQUISITIVE MINDS

it more than 30 times the length of the Grand Canyon! This astonishing feat of engineering snakes its way across China, protecting its borders for centuries.

> **EVER WONDERED WHAT IT'D BE LIKE TO** stand on top of the world? The Burj Khalifa in Dubai, UAE, completed in 2010, lets you do just that! At a jaw-dropping 828 (2726 feet) meters, it's the tallest building on Earth, dwarfing the Eiffel Tower by more than twice its height! Talk about reaching for the sky!

> **MARVEL AT THE AWE-INSPIRING SCALE OF** the international Space Station (ISS)! Orbiting Earth since 1998, this collaborative feat of engineering boasts a mass of 420,000 kilograms (925,000 pounds) and a habitable volume of 13,696 cubic feet (388 cubic meters). To put that in perspective, it's like a football field floating 250 miles above Earth!

> **WHAT IF A BRIDGE COULD LEAPFROG OVER** an entire island? The Hong Kong-Zhuhai-Macau Bridge, opened in 2018, is a 34-mile (55-kilometer) engineering marvel that connects the three cities. It's the world's longest sea-crossing bridge and includes a 4-mile (6.7-kilometer) underwater tunnel!

> **WHAT IF A BUILDING** resembled a blossoming lotus flower? The Lotus Temple in Delhi, india, completed in 1986, is a Bahá'í House of Worship. Its stunning design features 27 marble-clad petals arranged in groups of three, forming nine sides and nine entrances.

> **CAN YOU IMAGINE BUILDING SO WIDE THAT** it spans well over 12 football fields? The Boeing Everett Factory in Everett, Washington, completed in 1967, is the world's largest building by volume, encompassing an incredible 472 million cubic feet (13.3 million cubic meters) of space. It's where Boeing assembles its largest commercial airplanes.

> **DOES AN ISLAND BUILT ENTIRELY BY HUMANS** sound far-fetched? The Palm Jumeirah in Dubai, United Arab Emirates, completed in 2006, is a man-made island shaped like, you guessed it, a palm tree. It's so large it added 40 miles (64 kilometers) of coastline to Dubai, and astronuats have reported that it can even be seen from space!

> **HAVE YOU EVER HEARD OF A STRUCTURE THAT** can produce its own weather? The Eden Project in Cornwall, UK, completed in 2001, consists of two enormous biomes that house thousands of plant species. These domes are so massive that they create their own microclimates, with one replicating a tropical rainforest and the other a Mediterranean environment. It's like having the world's climates under one roof!

> **PICTURE AN AIRPORT SO IMMENSE IT COULD** fit 25 Vatican Cities inside it! The King Fahd international Airport in Dammam, Saudi Arabia, completed in 1999, covers a staggering 300 square miles (780 square kilometers) of land. Next time you're sprinting to catch a flight, remember: it could always be a longer run!

> **AN INDOOR SKI RESORT IN THE MIDDLE OF** the desert - say what?? Ski Dubai in the United Arab Emirates, opened in 2005, is the first indoor ski resort in

the Middle East, offering skiing, snowboarding, and even penguins. Who needs a winter wonderland when you've got your own snowy playground in the heat of summer!

> **IMAGINE AN UNDERWATER** hotel so luxurious it could make Atlantis green with envy! The Conrad Maldives Rangali Island in the Maldives opened the world's first underwater hotel suite, the Muraka, in 2018. Sleeping with the fishes never looked so glamorous!

> **WANT TO DRIVE ON THE WORLD'S HIGHEST** bridge? Head to China's Guizhou Province, where the Beipanjiang Bridge, completed in 2016, soars 565 meters above the Beipan River. That's taller than the Empire State Building! Don't look down if you're afraid of heights!

> **WHAT'S AS TALL AS A 15-STORY BUILDING,** weighs as much as 200 elephants, and moves at a snail's pace? The Bagger 293! This colossal bucket-wheel excavator, built in Germany in 1995, is the largest land vehicle on Earth. It's used to mine coal, and it can excavate an entire football field in just one day!

> **PICTURE A TELESCOPE SO MASSIVE THAT IT** could spot a fly on the Moon! The Five-hundred-meter Aperture Spherical Telescope (FAST) in China, completed in 2016, is the world's largest single-dish radio telescope. With a diameter of 1,640 feet (500 meters), it's as large as 30 football fields and helps scientists explore the mysteries of the universe.

> **IMAGINE A TUNNEL SO LONG IT COULD FIT** 267 Eiffel Towers end-to-end! The Gotthard Base Tunnel in Switzerland, completed in 2016, is the world's longest and deepest railway tunnel. It stretches for an astounding 35.5 miles (57 kilometers) and burrows more than 1.4 miles (2.3 kilometers) beneath the Swiss Alps. Talk about going the distance!

STORIES OF
WILD EXPERIMENTS

> **PICTURE THIS: A TWO-HEADED DOG! SOVIET** scientist Vladimir Demikhov shockingly created just that in 1954, transplanting a smaller dog's head onto a larger one. The duo survived for a month, making medical history in transplantation techniques.

> **IMAGINE A SCIENCE EXPERIMENT WHERE** cockroaches became mini-robots! in 2012, researchers at North Carolina State University created "Robo-Roaches" by attaching electronic backpacks to the insects. The backpacks allowed the scientists to control the roaches' movements, turning them into tiny, scuttling robots. Creepy or cool? You decide!

> **WHAT IF I TOLD YOU THAT ONE SCIENTIST** tried to make a human-chimpanzee hybrid? in the 1920s, Soviet biologist Ilya Ivanovich Ivanov attempted this bizarre experiment by artificially inseminating female chimps with human sperm. Unsurprisingly, the experiment failed, but it remains one of the craziest ideas in the history of science!

INCREDIBLE FACTS FOR INQUISITIVE MINDS

> **IMAGINE A SCIENTIST WHO WANTED** to teach dolphins to speak English! in the 1960s, neuroscientist John C. Lilly conducted an experiment where he attempted to teach dolphins human language by having a human live with them in a flooded house. Despite their best efforts, the dolphins never quite grasped the English language, but the experiment remains a fascinating tale of interspecies communication.

> **PICTURE A SCIENCE EXPERIMENT THAT AIMED** to create glow-in-the-dark pigs! in 2006, researchers in Taiwan successfully bred three pigs that glowed green under ultraviolet light. They injected pig embryos with jellyfish DNA, which produced a protein that made the pigs' skin and internal organs glow green. The goal of this bizarre experiment was to better understand the potential for genetically engineering animals for organ transplants and other medical purposes.

> **WHAT IF I TOLD YOU THERE WAS** a scientist who tried to create a "love potion" using sweat? in the 1990s, Claus Wedekind, a Swiss biologist, conducted a study known as the "sweaty T-shirt experiment." He asked male participants to wear a T-shirt for two days without deodorant and then had women rate the attractiveness of the scent. Surprisingly, the study found that women preferred the scent of men whose immune system genes were different from their own, suggesting that smell may play a role in mate selection.

> **IMAGINE A SCIENTIST WHO WANTED TO STUDY** the effects of isolation by living in a cave! in 1962, French geologist Michel Siffre spent two months living in complete isolation inside a subterranean cave with no access to clocks or sunlight. The aim of the experiment was to study how humans perceive time and adjust to extreme environments. Siffre's experience laid the groundwork for future research on circadian rhythms and the psychological effects of isolation.

> **DO SPIDERS GET HIGH?** in 1995, NASA scientists exposed spiders to different drugs and observed their web-weaving abilities. Turns out, caffeine makes spiders' webs a hot mess! This study provided unique insights into how drugs affect behavior across species.

> **WHAT IF YOUR POOP** could save the planet? in 2017, a team of scientists in Australia discovered a way to convert human waste into sustainable bricks. These eco-friendly building materials are not only stronger than traditional bricks but also reduce CO_2 emissions during production!

> **WHAT IF I TOLD YOU THAT RESEARCHERS** once attempted to use spiders to create a super-strong material? in 2012, a team of scientists at the University of Trento in Italy genetically modified silkworms to produce silk containing spider silk proteins. The resulting material was stronger, tougher, and more elastic than regular

silkworm silk. This experiment demonstrated the potential for creating innovative new materials using genetic engineering techniques.

> **WHAT ABOUT AN** experiment that involved testing the effects of a nuclear explosion on beer? in 1956, the United States Atomic Energy Commission conducted a study called "Operation Teapot" to determine the effects of a nuclear blast on various consumer goods, including bottled and canned beer. The results showed that,  despite some radioactive contamination, the beverages were still drinkable. This bizarre experiment highlighted the government's efforts to understand the potential consequences of nuclear warfare on everyday life.

> **WOULD YOU BELIEVE THAT SCIENTISTS ONCE** transformed a live cockroach into a remote-controlled "biobot" sporting a tiny electronic backpack? in 2012, the whizzes at North Carolina State University pulled off this astonishing feat with a Madagascar hissing cockroach, enabling them to steer the insect's movements from afar. The goal of this mind-boggling experiment was to assess the potential of insect cyborgs in search and rescue operations during disaster situations. Creepy-crawly tech has never been so electrifying!

CHAPTER TWO

POLITICAL PECULIARITIES

ECCENTRIC DICTATORS &
THE DARK SIDE OF POWER

> **VLADIMIR PUTIN'S PUBLIC PERSONA COULD** easily be the plot of a blockbuster movie. With a black belt in judo, a history as a KGB spy, fluency in multiple languages, potential presidential terms extending up to 30 years, and accusations of assassinating those that go against him, it's no doubt that he embodies a formidable character. His legend is further embellished by wild outdoor tales, such as once wrestling a bear in the Siberian wilderness. While some stories may blur the line between fact and folklore, they definitely enhance his strongman image among his people.

> **WHAT DO YOU GET WHEN YOU MIX** a dictator, a harem, and a penchant for lavish parties? Muammar Gaddafi, the infamous Libyan leader from 1969 to 2011, known for his eccentric fashion sense and bizarre antics, had a harem of women bodyguards who were required to dress in military-style uniforms and wear makeup. Seems like Gaddafi took "girl power" to a whole new level.

> **WOULD YOU BELIEVE A DICTATOR COULD BE** so paranoid that he'd order the execution of his own family members? Iraq's Saddam Hussein, who ruled from 1979 to 2003, brother-in-law and uncle killed after they defected and then returned to Iraq. Talk about taking family drama to a whole new level!

INCREDIBLE FACTS FOR INQUISITIVE MINDS

> **HOW ABOUT A DICTATOR SO VAIN,**
he renamed months after himself? Turkmenistan's
Saparmurat Niyazov, who ruled from 1991 to 2006,
renamed January after himself and April after
his mother. That's one way to make sure
your legacy lives on!

> **CAN A DICTATOR BE SO**
feared that he'd poison his own people?
Zimbabwe's Robert Mugabe, who
ruled from 1980 to 2017, was accused
of poisoning the opposition leader in
2017. This sinister act shows that
nothing is off-limits when it comes to
maintaining power.

> **WHO KNEW A DICTATOR COULD**
be a Disney fan? Romania's Nicolae Ceausescu, who ruled
from 1965 to 1989, loved Disney so much that he had a
replica of Disneyland built in his country. However, the
theme park was only accessible to the elite, leaving the
average Romanian citizen in the cold.

> **EVER HEARD OF A DICTATOR WHO FANCIED**
himself a poet? Uganda's Idi Amin, who ruled from
1971 to 1979, wrote poetry and even released an album.
However, his artistic pursuits didn't make up for the
300,000 deaths he caused during his brutal reign.

> **CAN YOU IMAGINE A DICTATOR WITH A SOFT**
spot for animals? Benito Mussolini, Italy's dictator from
1922 to 1943, was known to keep a pet lion named Ras
in his office. It's a stark contrast to the millions of
lives lost during his rule and alliance with Hitler during
World War II.

> **DID YOU KNOW THAT ADOLF HITLER,**
the infamous dictator of Nazi Germany (1933-1945),
was a vegetarian and an animal lover? While he
masterminded the Holocaust, resulting in the deaths
of millions, Hitler despised hunting and even passed
laws to protect animals. Talk about a contradiction!

> **WHO WOULD HAVE GUESSED THAT JOSEPH**
Stalin, the iron-fisted ruler of the Soviet Union
(1924-1953), had a penchant for colored pencils?
As he orchestrated the Great Purge and the forced
collectivization of farms, causing millions to perish,
Stalin doodled and annotated official documents with
a rainbow of colored pencils. Artistic tyranny, anyone?

> **KIM JONG-IL, NORTH KOREA'S ECCENTRIC**
dictator (1994-2011), was a massive cinephile! He owned
a collection of over 20,000 films while his people suffered
from starvation and poverty. Kim even kidnapped a South
Korean director and actress in 1978 to improve North
Korea's film industry. Talk about an extreme movie buff!

> **BENITO MUSSOLINI, ITALY'S INFAMOUS**
fascist dictator (1925-1943), wrote a bodice-ripper novel?
As he led Italy into World War II and brutally suppressed
dissent, Il Duce penned "The Cardinal's Mistress," which
was published in 1925. Who knew he had a soft spot
for romance?

> **PICTURE THIS: THE INFAMOUS DICTATOR**
responsible for the Cambodian Genocide had a love for...
horticulture? Pol Pot, the leader of the Khmer Rouge in
the 1970s, adored gardening and tended to his plants
with great care, despite causing the deaths of nearly

2 million people. It's hard to imagine such a ruthless individual finding solace in nurturing something as delicate as a flower.

> **DID YOU KNOW THE MAN WHO SPEARHEADED** the Cuban Revolution had a thing for dairy products? Fidel Castro, the communist leader of Cuba from 1959 to 2008, was so enamored with ice cream that he built an ice cream parlor in Havana, capable of holding 1,000 customers. The mind reels at the contrast between his revolutionary zeal and his love for a sweet, frozen treat.

> **CAN YOU FATHOM A BRUTAL** dictator being a connoisseur of fine cheese? North Korea's Kim Jong-un, the supreme leader since 2011, reportedly imports luxurious Swiss cheeses to satisfy his gourmet cravings. As his citizens suffer from malnutrition and poverty, Kim Jong-un indulges in a cheesy feast, making his passion for dairy a jarring contradiction to his oppressive rule.

> **IMAGINE A DICTATOR WITH** a penchant for ballet? Mao Zedong, the founding father of the People's Republic of China, was a massive fan of the art form. Despite initiating the Cultural Revolution in the 1960s and causing the deaths of millions, Mao found solace in the grace and beauty of ballet. It's perplexing to think that a man who orchestrated such suffering could find peace in such an elegant pursuit.

> **CAN YOU BELIEVE A DICTATOR'S LOVE FOR** basketball led to an unlikely friendship? Kim Jong-un, North Korea's supreme leader, is a die-hard basketball fan with a special fondness for the NBA. His passion for the sport is so strong that in 2013, he invited former NBA star Dennis Rodman to visit North Korea. The two formed an improbable bond, leaving us to ponder the power of sports in bridging even the most unlikely of connections.

> **WOULD IT SHOCK YOU TO LEARN THAT** a ruthless dictator was a devoted animal lover? Francisco Franco, who ruled Spain with an iron grip from 1939 to 1975, had a soft spot for furry friends. He adored his pet Persian cat so much that he reportedly let it sleep on his bed. While Franco's regime was characterized by repression and brutality, his affection for his feline companion shows a different side to his persona.

> **PICTURE THIS:** a feared African dictator who couldn't resist the charm of a popular French song. Mobutu Sese Seko, who ruled Zaire (now the Democratic Republic of Congo) from 1965 to 1997, loved the tune "La Vie en Rose" by Édith Piaf. He even played the song on a loop in his presidential palace. It's fascinating to think that a man responsible for widespread human rights abuses could find solace in a romantic French ballad.

> **DID YOU KNOW THAT THE SELF-PROCLAIMED** Emperor of the Central African Republic had a passion for haute couture? Jean-Bédel Bokassa, who ruled from

1966 to 1979, spent a fortune on his coronation ceremony, modeling it after Napoleon Bonaparte's. He donned a lavish, custom-made robe adorned with 785,000 pearls and diamonds. It's mind-boggling to consider the opulence of such an event in contrast to the poverty experienced by his people.

> **CAN YOU WRAP YOUR HEAD AROUND THE FACT** that the former dictator of Iraq had a soft spot for romance novels? Saddam Hussein, while responsible for countless atrocities, penned a romantic novel titled "Zabibah and the King." The novel, published in 2000, tells the story of a love affair between a ruler and a commoner, providing a bizarre glimpse into the dictator's more sentimental side.

> **AN IRON FIST LEADER WITH A GREEN THUMB?** Benito Mussolini, Italy's fascist dictator from 1922 to 1943, was an avid gardener who found respite in tending to his plants. While Mussolini's regime was characterized by war and brutality, his love for nature showed a contrasting, more peaceful side to his personality.

> **IMAGINE AN AFRICAN DICTATOR WITH A KILT** collection. Idi Amin, Uganda's notorious leader, had an unusual fascination with Scotland, going as far as declaring himself the King of Scotland. While his rule was marked by terror and human rights abuses, Amin's odd connection to Scottish culture adds an unexpected layer to his infamous legacy

> **WHEN YOUR HORSE IS YOUR DRINKING BUDDY.** Bolivian President Mariano Melgarejo was known for his eccentricity, famously once forcing his horse to drink beer during official receptions. This bizarre act was a mere footnote in a presidency characterized by folly and misrule, leading to national turmoil and his eventual overthrow.

> **WITH A STEADFAST NO-ALCOHOL RULE,**
Trump has a fizzy vice of choice—Diet Coke! He's such an
aficionado that he often guzzles down a whopping 12 cans
in a single day.

> **IN KIM JONG-UN'S REGIME, EVEN A TINY**
slip like nodding off in a meeting could lead to big trouble.
One official found this out the hard way when he was
reportedly executed with anti-aircraft weapon for
catching some zzz's during a meeting.

> **THE NORTH KOREAN LEADER'S METHOD OF**
getting rid of rivals—or anyone he thinks is a rival—isn't
to be taken lightly. Rumor has it that in 2012, he had a
former army vice minister blown up with a mortar for
partying too hard after Kim's dad died. His uncle, Jang
Song Thaek, supposedly ended up naked and thrown to 120
hungry dogs in 2013.

WEIRD LAWS & LEGISLATION FROM AROUND THE WORLD

> **CAN YOU IMAGINE BEING FINED FOR NOT**
walking your dog thrice a day? in Turin, Italy, dog owners
who fail to walk their furry friends at least three times
a day can be fined up to €500! That's a lot of pasta!
Pooches in Turin are surely living la dolce vita.

> **REMEMBER THAT CHILDHOOD GAME, "DON'T STEP**
on a crack"? in Carmel, California, you'd better take it
seriously. Wearing high heels over 2 inches in height without
a permit is illegal! This quirky law was enacted to prevent

lawsuits from accidents caused by Carmel's irregular pavement. So, ladies and gents, make sure you've got your permit before you strut your stuff!

> DO YOU HAVE A HANKERING FOR A MIDNIGHT

snack? Beware if you're in Switzerland! It's illegal to flush the toilet after 10 PM in an apartment building. The Swiss consider it noise pollution! Talk about an inconvenient truth for those with a weak bladder.

> LOVEBIRDS, TAKE NOTE! IN EBOLI, ITALY,

smooching in a moving vehicle is illegal. If caught locking lips behind the wheel, you could be slapped with a fine of up to €500! So, save the romance for a sunset stroll or a candlelit dinner, not the open road.

> ARE YOU A FAN OF WINNIE-THE-POOH?

You'd better keep it on the down-low in Tuszyn, Poland! This cuddly bear was banned as a mascot for a local playground, as officials deemed him "inappropriately dressed" due to his lack of pants. Sorry, Pooh Bear, it seems you're just too risqué for the kiddos!

> CHICKENS, BEWARE!

in Quitman, Georgia, it's illegal for a chicken to cross the road. No, we're not kidding! This law was put in place keep farm animals off the streets and protect motorists. Sadly, we may never know why the chicken wanted to cross the road in the first place.

> HAVE A SWEET TOOTH?

in Derby, Kansas, it's illegal to hit a vending machine when it fails to release your candy. This quirky law aims to prevent people from damaging the machines in a fit of frustration. So, if you're hankering for a candy bar, you'd better be prepared to play nice with the vending machine!

> ARE YOU A FAN OF GOLDFISH? IN MONZA,

Italy, it's illegal to keep them in a bowl! This seemingly bizarre law was enacted to promote animal welfare, as goldfish bowls don't provide adequate space and oxygen for these little swimmers. So, if you want to keep a goldfish in Monza, you'd better upgrade to a more spacious tank!

> ARE YOU AN AVID GUM CHEWER?

You might want to skip visiting Singapore! The sale of chewing gum is strictly prohibited in this city-state. This law was introduced to maintain cleanliness and orderliness in public spaces. So, if you're craving a chewy treat, you'll have to settle for a mint instead!

> ARE YOU A FAN OF ARCADE

games? in South Carolina, it's illegal for anyone under the age of 18 to play pinball. This bewildering law was enacted to keep youngsters from wasting their time and money on frivolous pursuits. Sorry, kids, you'll have to find another way to test your reflexes and hand-eye coordination!

> FANCY YOURSELF A DAREDEVIL CYCLIST?

in Mexico City, it's illegal to ride your bike while lifting both feet off the pedals. This law aims to ensure the safety of cyclists and pedestrians by preventing reckless behavior. So, if you're planning to pop a wheelie or perform some fancy footwork, you'd better think twice!

> **LOVE SNACKING ON PICKLES? IN TRENTON,** New Jersey, it's illegal to eat a pickle on Sunday. This bizarre law dates back to the days of strict Sunday observance, which prohibited various activities, including the consumption of pickles. So, if you're craving a crunchy treat, you'd better wait until Monday rolls around!

> **IN MELBOURNE, AUSTRALIA, IT'S ILLEGAL** to vacuum your house between 10 PM and 7 AM on weekdays and between 10 PM and 9 AM on weekends. This noise-restricting law aims to promote peace and quiet for residents, ensuring a good night's sleep for all. So, if you're planning a late-night cleaning spree, you'd better use your superpowers to keep the noise down!

> **IN 18TH CENTURY RUSSIA, PETER THE GREAT** imposed a beard tax on his subjects. Men who wished to keep their whiskers had to pay a hefty sum for a special token, which they had to carry as proof of payment. Clean-shaven faces were all the rage in the Russian court, but we can't help but wonder how many burly beards were lost to this peculiar policy!

> **LOVE A GOOD GAME OF SOCCER?** in 14th century England, King Edward II banned the sport, as it was seen as a distraction from more important activities, such as archery practice. Soccer enthusiasts had to wait more than 300 years for the ban to be lifted! It's hard to imagine a world without the beautiful game.

> **DO YOU ENJOY A GOOD GOSSIP SESSION?** in ancient Rome, gossiping was considered a crime! If you were caught spreading rumors or sharing juicy tidbits about your neighbors, you could be punished with a hefty fine or even banishment. So, if you lived in ancient Rome, you'd better have kept your lips sealed and your secrets to yourself!

> **IN MEDIEVAL ENGLAND, IT WAS ILLEGAL**
to wear certain colors or fabrics based on your social
status. Sumptuary laws dictated what each class could
wear, preventing commoners from dressing above their
station. It's a good thing we're no longer limited by these
fashion faux pas, as we'd have a tough time deciding
what to wear!

> **CAN YOU IMAGINE HAVING TO PAY A FINE**
for wearing a hat? in ancient Athens, it was illegal for
women to wear hats outside of their homes. This curious
law was enacted to prevent women from appearing taller
than men and to maintain the social hierarchy of the
time. Thankfully, fashion freedom has come a long way
since then!

> **ARE YOU A FAN OF AFTERNOON NAPS?**
in 15th century Florence, Italy, it was illegal to nap
in the afternoon. Authorities believed that daytime
snoozing led to laziness and immoral behavior. Luckily,
modern society has embraced the concept of siestas,
allowing us to catch some much-needed Zs in the
middle of the day!

> **IN ANCIENT EGYPT, IT WAS ILLEGAL TO KILL**
a cat, even accidentally! Cats were considered sacred
animals and were often associated with the goddess
Bastet. Killing a cat, even unintentionally, could result
in severe penalties, including death. It's clear that the
ancient Egyptians were true cat lovers!

> **IN ANCIENT CHINA, IT WAS ILLEGAL FOR**
commoners to wear the color yellow. This vibrant hue
was reserved for the emperor and his family, symbolizing
their power and status. Breaking this law could result

in severe penalties, including confiscation of property and even execution. Today, we're free to wear any color of the rainbow without fear of reprisal! Can you imagine being punished for wearing the wrong shoes? .

> **ARE YOU A FAN OF FACIAL HAIR?** IN ANCIENT Persia, it was illegal for men to shave their beards! Beards were considered a symbol of wisdom and manliness, and shaving them was seen as a sign of disgrace. So, if you lived in ancient Persia, you'd better have been prepared to embrace your inner lumberjack!

> IN MEDIEVAL **GERMANY,** IT WAS ILLEGAL to dance during the entire season of Lent. This somber period leading up to Easter was meant to be a time of reflection and self-discipline. Dancing was seen as a frivolous and sinful activity, so anyone caught breaking this law could face severe penalties, including fines and public shaming.

A LOOK INTO THE SECRET WORLD OF MONARCHIES

> **CAN YOU IMAGINE WEARING A WIG MADE** of mouse fur? Well, in 18th-century France, Queen Marie Antoinette had a penchant for these strange hairpieces. Yep, you heard it right—mouse fur! She flaunted these furry wonders in the opulent Palace of Versailles, and her unusual taste in wigs soon became the talk of the town. Imagine the surprise of her subjects when they discovered their queen's odd choice of headwear!

> **LET'S TIME-TRAVEL TO THE 16TH-CENTURY**
Ottoman Empire, where Sultan Ibrahim the Mad ruled with
an iron (and incredibly eccentric) fist. This quirky ruler
loved his pets, but he took his passion to the extreme.
He would fill the palace gardens in Istanbul with giraffes,
lions, and even a humongous elephant! Can you imagine the
chaos and the smell? We bet the gardeners were less than
thrilled about their daily duties.

> **HAVE YOU EVER WONDERED HOW FAR**
someone would go for fashion? King Henry VIII of England,
who reigned in the early 16th century, had a "thing" for
codpieces. These were padded pouches that covered his
royal jewels, and he made sure they were not only large but
also elaborately decorated. Imagine the courtiers trying
to keep a straight face as the king strutted around in his
extravagant attire!

> **IN 1953, QUEEN SIRIKIT OF THAILAND**
decided to give the world's most expensive omelet
a whirl. This luxurious dish, prepared in the royal palace
in Bangkok, contained a jaw-dropping 465 eggs and was
garnished with lobster, truffle, and edible gold leaf.
Can you fathom the size of that frying pan? We can't help
but wonder what the royal chef thought of this lavish
culinary endeavor.

> **PICTURE THIS: IT'S 17TH-CENTURY SWEDEN,**
and Queen Christina is ruling the roost. Known for her
unconventional ways, she loved to ride her horse through
the halls of her Stockholm palace! Imagine the surprise of
her courtiers, dodging hooves left and right. Talk about
a royal entrance!

> **EVER HEARD OF A KING WITH A NOSE FOR** perfume? in the 18th century, King George IV of England had an insatiable appetite for fine scents. He'd order a whopping 1,000 bottles of perfume per year! Just think about the air in the royal palace—enough to make anyone swoon!

> **LET'S HOP ACROSS THE POND** to the Hawaiian Kingdom, where King Kamehameha III ruled in the mid-19th century. This fun-loving monarch loved to surf—on planks made of solid koa wood! How's that for a royal beach day? We bet his subjects wished they could join in the fun!

> **CAN YOU IMAGINE** having a pet bear at your beck and call? in the early 16th century, Catherine de' Medici, the Queen of France, had her very own live bear! She'd parade this ferocious creature around the French court in Paris, giving her guests a real shock.

> **HERE'S A TIDBIT FROM 14TH-CENTURY MALI:** Mansa Musa, the wealthiest man in history, had a penchant for gold—so much so that he would distribute it to the poor during his legendary pilgrimage to Mecca. Imagine the awe of the people who received these golden gifts!

> **IN 18TH-CENTURY SPAIN, KING CHARLES III** loved to dress up as a commoner and wander the streets of Madrid incognito. Picture the bafflement of his subjects when they discovered the king in their midst, dressed like an ordinary Joe!

> **SULTAN MURAD IV OF THE 17TH-CENTURY**
Ottoman Empire enforced an unusual law. He banned
coffee, believing it was causing social unrest in Istanbul!
Can you imagine the grumpiness of caffeine-deprived
subjects? We bet the mornings were rough!

> **ANCIENT EGYPTIAN QUEEN CLEOPATRA HAD**
a penchant for pearls. Legend has it she dissolved one
in vinegar and drank it to win a bet with her lover,
Mark Antony! Just think about the opulence of that
cocktail. Cheers to extravagance!

> **IMAGINE A MONARCH WITH 357 PIERCINGS!**
King Cetshwayo of the Zulu Kingdom in 19th-century South
Africa sported these adornments as a symbol of power.

> **DID YOU KNOW THAT QUEEN ISABELLA I**
of Spain, who reigned in the late 15th century, claimed she'd
only bathed twice in her life? Imagine the royal court trying
to hold their breath as they went about their duties!

> **IN 18TH-CENTURY PRUSSIA, KING FREDERICK**
the Great was obsessed with tall soldiers. He even created
an elite regiment of towering troops called the "Potsdam
Giants"! Can you picture these lofty warriors marching
through the streets of Berlin?

> **EMPRESS ELISABETH OF AUSTRIA, ALSO**
known as Sisi, was a 19th-century beauty icon. She had an
intense hair care routine, which included using raw eggs
and cognac as a conditioner! Can you imagine the smell
in the Habsburg palace as she brushed her tresses?

> **LET'S HEAD TO ANCIENT EGYPT, WHERE**
Cleopatra VII, the last Pharaoh, was rumored to bathe
in donkey milk. She believed it kept her skin youthful and

beautiful. Can you picture the sheer absurdity of an entire herd of donkeys being milked just for her royal baths? No wonder her subjects were less than thrilled!

> **HER MAJESTY QUEEN ELIZABETH II**
wasn't just sovereign of the nation; she was the proud patron of a pack of Pembroke Welsh corgis. This regal affair began with a corgi named Dookie in her childhood and grew to over 30 corgis throughout her lifetime, each trotting through the palace corridors with the grace of canine royalty.

> **THE QUEEN HAD A FLEET OF CARS**
and wasn't just a figurehead; she took the wheel with gusto. Elizabeth II served as a mechanic and a truck driver during World War II, skills that gave her a mechanical mastery unlike any other monarch.

SECRET OPERATIONS YOU DIDN'T KNOW HAPPENED

> **CAN YOU IMAGINE A REAL-LIFE JAMES**
Bond? Meet Sidney Reilly, the British "Ace of Spies"! Born in 1873, this Russian-born adventurer worked for British intelligence and was involved in countless clandestine operations. The most unbelievable part? Reilly played a pivotal role in the attempted assassination of Vladimir Lenin in 1918. Though he didn't succeed, his legendary exploits inspired Ian Fleming's iconic secret agent.

> **WORLD WAR II, 1943,** AND AN AMERICAN plan so daring, it boggles the mind! Operation Mincemeat involved the British dressing up a corpse as a high-ranking military officer, complete with fake documents. They let the body wash up on a Spanish beach to trick the Germans into believing the Allies would invade Greece, not Sicily. Spoiler alert: the ruse worked, and the Germans diverted resources away from the real target!

> **DID YOU KNOW A HUMBLE HOUSEWIFE COULD** change the course of war? in 1941, British housewife and secret agent Virginia Hall worked for the Special Operations Executive (SOE) in Nazi-occupied France. With a wooden leg and nerves of steel, she coordinated the French Resistance, paving the way for the Allies' D-Day invasion. The Nazis called her "the most dangerous of all Allied spies" – talk about girl power!

> **WHAT IF I TOLD YOU A FAKE TOWN HELPED** win the Cold War? in 1980s America, a top-secret operation called Project Azorian aimed to recover a sunken Soviet submarine from the Pacific Ocean floor. The CIA built a fictitious mining company, complete with a fake town, just to conceal their real mission! The operation, though partially successful, remains one of the most audacious and expensive covert missions in history.

> **EVER HEARD OF A WEAPONIZED DOLPHIN?** in the 1960s, the U.S. Navy Marine Mammal Program trained dolphins and sea lions for covert missions! These cute-yet-deadly creatures were taught to detect underwater mines and even plant explosives on enemy vessels. It's rumored that the Soviet Union also had a similar program. Flipper, is that you?

> **WHAT IF YOUR FAVORITE BOARD GAME HELD**
a secret? During World War II, the British intelligence
agency MI9 collaborated with the creators of Monopoly
to help Allied prisoners escape from Nazi POW camps.
They hid silk maps, compasses, and real money within the
game's components! Unbeknownst to their captors,
prisoners received these life-saving tools, cleverly disguised
as innocent entertainment.

> **EVER WONDERED IF AN UMBRELLA COULD BE**
deadly? in 1978, Georgi Markov, a Bulgarian activist,
was assassinated in London by an agent using a modified
umbrella. The umbrella fired a tiny, poison-filled pellet
into Markov's leg as he walked across Waterloo Bridge.
It was later revealed that the KGB and the Bulgarian
secret service collaborated on this cold-blooded
assassination, sending chills down the spine of anyone
wielding a brolly.

> **WHO KNEW PIGEONS COULD BE SECRET AGENTS?**
During World War I and II, British intelligence employed
homing pigeons to carry vital messages across enemy lines.
These brave and unsung heroes of the sky saved countless
lives by transporting encrypted messages between spies,
resistance fighters, and the military. One feathered friend,
named Mary of Exeter, even survived multiple injuries
in the line of duty, proving that espionage knows no species!

> **IN THE 1960s, THE U.S. INTELLIGENCE**
agency embarked on "Operation Acoustic Kitty," a bizarre
plan to eavesdrop on Soviet conversations. They implanted
microphones and radio transmitters inside cats and sent
them to prowl near the Soviets. Alas, the project was
short-lived, as feline spies proved to be, well, less than
cooperative. Talk about a purr-fect disaster!

> **EVER HEARD OF AN INVISIBLE INK RECIPE**
written by a Founding Father? George Washington,
America's first president, was also a spymaster during
the Revolutionary War. Washington oversaw the Culper
Spy Ring, a network of American spies who used invisible
ink, coded messages, and even laundry lines to communicate
vital intelligence. The invisible ink recipe, concocted by
Washington himself, was later used by the CIA during
the Cold War.

> **JUAN PUJOL GARCÍA, A SPANISH NATIONAL,**
played a crucial role in the success of the D-Day invasion
in 1944. He fed the Nazis false information about the
Allies' invasion plans, all while working for the British.
His deception was so masterful that he was awarded
medals by both the Germans and the British – talk about
playing both sides of the fence!

> **DID YOU KNOW A LEGENDARY JAZZ MUSICIAN**
was once an undercover agent? During World War II,
American jazz trumpeter Louis Armstrong secretly worked
for the U.S. Office of Strategic Services (OSS), the CIA's
predecessor. Armstrong used his international fame to
gather intelligence while touring Europe and Africa. Who
knew the man behind "What a Wonderful World" was also
part of a high-stakes world of intrigue?

> **CAN YOU BELIEVE THAT AN ORDINARY–LOOKING**
rock hid a high-tech secret? in 2006, Russian television
revealed a fake rock containing a hidden electronic device,
used by British spies to transmit and receive information.
Placed in a Moscow park, this seemingly innocuous stone was
a cutting-edge tool in the world of espionage. It's enough to
make you wonder what secrets might be hiding beneath your
garden rocks!

> **EVER HEARD OF A SPY WHO SAVED THE WORLD**
from nuclear annihilation? Vasili Arkhipov, a Soviet naval
officer, was the unsung hero of the Cuban Missile Crisis.
In 1962, aboard a submarine that lost contact with Moscow,
Arkhipov refused to authorize a nuclear torpedo launch
against the U.S. fleet. His courageous decision prevented
a catastrophic escalation of the crisis and a potential nuclear
war. Hats off to Arkhipov, a true spy for peace!

> **WHAT IF YOUR FAVORITE AUTHOR WAS ALSO**
a top-secret spy? Roald Dahl, the beloved British author of
children's classics like "Charlie and the Chocolate Factory"
and "Matilda," was also an undercover agent during World
War II. Working for the British Security Coordination
in Washington, D.C., Dahl used his charm and wit to gather
intelligence from high-ranking U.S. officials. It seems
there's more to this wordsmith than meets the eye!

> **EVER HEARD OF A SECRET AGENT WHO WAS ALSO**
a world-famous chef? Julia Child, the beloved American
chef, and TV personality, was a covert operative for the
Office of Strategic Services (OSS) during World War II.
Child worked on projects like developing shark repellent and
creating a recipe for a deadly, odorless poison. Who knew the
queen of French cuisine had such a hidden past?

> **PICTURE A SPY OPERATION SO BIZARRE,**
it involved a magician's trick! in 1953, the CIA enlisted
the help of magician John Mulholland to develop
sleight-of-hand techniques for covertly drugging targets.
The project, known as MK-ULTRA, aimed to explore
mind control and chemical interrogation methods using
psychoactive drugs. This collaboration between a master
illusionist and the CIA proves that sometimes truth is
stranger than fiction!

CHAPTER THREE

STELLAR
SPACE SECRETS

THE WONDERS OF OUTER SPACE

> **PREPARE FOR LIFT-OFF WITH THIS** mind-boggling **fact** that will give you a sense of just how vast our known reality is: there are an estimated 100 billion galaxies in the observable universe! That's like having a galaxy for every grain of sand on Earth's beaches and then some.

> **DID YOU KNOW THAT OUR VERY OWN** Milky Way galaxy is on a collision course with our cosmic neighbor, the Andromeda galaxy? Fear not; this cataclysmic event won't take place for another 4.5 billion years...a lot can happen in that time. We'll most likely be living on another planet (or multiple) by then!

> **THE LARGEST KNOWN STAR, UY SCUTI,** is a massive 1,700 times larger than our Sun. If you placed UY Scuti in our solar system, it would stretch from the Sun all the way to Jupiter—now that's a HUGE celestial fireball!

> **THE NEAREST STAR TO EARTH,** Proxima Centauri, is 4.24 light-years away—to put that into perspective, on a commercial airplane maintaining a constant average speed, it would take about 6.3 million years to get there. Now that's what I call a long-haul flight!

INCREDIBLE FACTS FOR INQUISITIVE MINDS

> **IMAGINE A COSMIC** waterfall of pure energy cascading across the universe. Quasars, powered by supermassive black holes, are the brightest objects in the universe. They emit enormous amounts of energy, equivalent to the light of a trillion suns!

> **HERE IS A COSMIC CURIOSITY: STARS DON'T** actually twinkle in the sky. The "twinkling" of light in the night sky we see from Earth is caused by turbulence in Earth's atmosphere scattering the starlight, creating the sparkling illusion. It's like Mother Nature has her own special effects team!

> **EVER WONDERED WHERE ALL THE GOLD IN THE** universe comes from? It's made in the heart of a stellar explosion known as a supernova! When massive stars die, they create heavy elements like gold, silver, and platinum. So, next time you wear a gold necklace, remember you're donning a piece of cosmic bling forged in the fiery furnace of a dying star.

> **HERE'S A GALACTIC JAW-DROPPER OF A FACT:** A neutron star, formed from the collapsed core of a larger star, is so dense that just one sugar-cube-sized portion of its material would weigh a bizarre 100 million tons on Earth! That's heavier than the entire population of nearly eight billion humans combined.

> **A SUPERNOVA, THE EXPLOSION OF A DYING** star, will briefly outshine an entire galaxy! These cosmic fireworks release more energy in a moment than our Sun will release in its entire 10-billion-year lifetime. Talk about going out with a bang!

> **IF YOU COMBINED THE BRIGHTNESS OF ALL** the stars together visible from Earth, a full Moon would still be 40 times brighter. No wonder poets (and werewolves alike) find it so captivating!

> **SOME FAR-OUT THEORIES SUGGEST THAT** Earth's precious water might have originated from comets or perhaps even an ancient alien civilization. Our oceans could be the result of an intergalactic ice delivery service – just without the cocktail to go with it! Next time you take a sip of water, remember you might be enjoying a cosmic drink resulting from extraterrestrial intervention.

> **PICTURE A GIANT COSMIC DIAMOND,** sparkling like a celestial gemstone! Meet BPM 37093, a white dwarf star estimated to have a crystallized carbon core equivalent (aka a massive diamond) to 10 billion trillion trillion carats. Scientists believe that the immense pressure and temperature within the star caused the carbon atoms to organize into a diamond-like crystalline lattice. Located about 50 light-years away from Earth in the constellation Centaurus, this "diamond star" is an extravagant reminder of the universe's ability to create astonishing phenomena.

> **THINK OUR MILKY WAY GALAXY IS MASSIVE?** Wait until you hear about IC 1101, the largest known galaxy in the observable universe! Located a whopping 1 billion

light-years away in the constellation Serpens, IC 1101 is a mind-bending 6 million light-years across. To put that into perspective, it would take our Sun 225 million years to travel just 1% of that distance! IC 1101 is so enormous that it contains about 100 trillion stars, enough to create 10,000 Milky Way-sized galaxies. Now that's what we call a cosmic heavyweight!

> CAN YOU IMAGINE WINDS SO FIERCE THAT they whip up shards of glass and send them hurtling sideways? Well, that's precisely what happens on HD 189733b, a blazing-hot exoplanet located 63 light-years away from Earth! This alien world experiences winds that reach up to 5,400 miles per hour (8,700 kilometers per hour) and temperatures of around 1,700 degrees Fahrenheit (930 degrees Celsius). The intense heat causes silicate particles in the atmosphere to condense and form glass. The ferocious winds then pick up these glass shards and fling them horizontally, creating a terrifying storm of glass projectiles. It's safe to say this is one place you'd want to avoid on your interstellar travels!

ODDITIES OF OUR SOLAR SYSTEM & BEYOND

> MERCURY IS THE SMALLEST PLANET IN OUR solar system—it has a very peculiar day-night cycle. Its slow rotation and rapid orbit around the Sun means a single day on Mercury lasts about 58.6 Earth days, while only 88 Earth days make up a year! Imagine celebrating your birthday every three months, what fun!

> **MARS'S TWO SMALL MOONS, PHOBOS AND**
Deimos, are oddly shaped and resemble potatoes! Some
scientists believe that these peculiar satellites might be
captured asteroids from the asteroid belt. Phobos means
fear, Deimos means terror, and Mars is named after
the Roman God of war. Now that's quite a lot of feisty
space rocks.

> **ALTHOUGH MARS IS KNOWN AS THE**
Red Planet, its sunsets appear blue due to the way
sunlight scatters through the thin Martian atmosphere.
As the Sun dips below the horizon, future settlers will
enjoy a spectacular cosmic light show, unlike anything
seen on Earth.

> **OUR AMAZING SUN IS ACTUALLY NOT**
yellow, but white! Our star only appears yellow to us here
because of Planet Earth's atmosphere, which scatters
sunlight, filtering out various colors. If you were to
observe the Sun from outer space (with proper protection,
of course), you'd see it in all its radiant, white glory!

> **ON VENUS, IT RAINS**
sulfuric acid - while on Uranus,
you might experience a rain of
diamonds! High-pressure
experiments have suggested
that the intense heat and
pressure in the ice giant's
atmosphere could cause carbon
atoms to form diamonds, which
would then fall like rain toward
the planet's core. Talk about
a dazzling downpour!

INCREDIBLE FACTS FOR INQUISITIVE MINDS

> **MARS BOASTS THE LARGEST VOLCANO IN THE**
solar system—called Olympus Mons. It's 13.6 miles
(22 kilometers) high and 370 miles (600 kilometers)
in diameter. That's about three times higher than
Mount Everest!

> **URANUS IS AN UNUSUAL PLANET THAT**
rotates on its side. Its extreme tilt may have been
caused by a massive collision with an Earth-sized comet,
giving it a unique orientation, with its poles in 42 years
of continuous sunlight followed by 42 years of darkness.
Now that's what we call a long day!

> **THE MOON IS DRIFTING AWAY FROM EARTH**
at a rate of 1.48 inches (3.8 centimeters) per year! Don't
worry though—it'll actually take billions of years before it
makes any significant difference to our tides, eclipses, and
life here on Earth. Phew!

> **CAN YOU BELIEVE THAT OUR MOON HAS...**
moonquakes! Caused by the gravitational interaction with
Earth, these quakes are far less powerful than their
Earthy counterparts, but they can still make the Moon's
surface rumble and shake!

> **DID YOU KNOW THAT THE SUN'S CORE**
temperature is a sizzling 27 million degrees Fahrenheit
(15 million degrees Celsius)! Summer temperatures on
planet Earth seem tame in comparison!

> **THE SPEED OF LIGHT TRAVELS AT 186,282**
miles per second (299,792 kilometers per second)
in a vacuum. That's like going around Earth's equator
over seven times in just one second!

> **EVER HEARD OF THE COSMIC SPEED LIMIT?**
in our universe, science has concluded that nothing can
travel faster than the speed of light. According to
Einstein's theory of relativity, as an object approaches
the speed of light, its mass increases, requiring more and
more energy to keep accelerating. Only massless particles,
which make up light, can travel at that speed.

> **HERE IS A PHOTON FUN FACT! LIGHT SLOWS**
down a bit when it travels through a medium like water or
glass. This speed reduction causes light to bend or refract,
which then leads to optical illusions we see, like mirages
and rainbows.

> **HERE'S A FACT ABOUT STARLIGHT THAT YOU**
might not know: the light we see from distant stars took
quite a long time to reach us. The nearest star to Earth,
Proxima Centauri, is about 4.24 light-years away, meaning
the light we see from it now actually started its journey
to Earth over four years ago. When we look up, we are
literally looking into the past!

> **DUE TO THE COSMIC SPEED LIMIT,**
astronauts traveling at high speeds relative to Earth may
find themselves in something of a time warp (no, not the
dance from "Rocky Horror"!). Thanks to time dilation, the
faster you move, the slower time passes for you compared
to a stationary being. Clocks in airplanes tick at different
rates from clocks on the ground. So, if you go for a trip
on a super-fast spaceship, you might return home actually
younger than your Earth-bound twin.

> **IF YOU THINK YOUR LAST ROAD TRIP WAS**
long, try traveling to Mars! It takes about 9 months to
get there—roughly the same amount of time it takes for

a baby to be born. And once you arrive, you'd better like red because Mars, named after the Roman God of war, is often called the "Red Planet" due to its reddish appearance from the iron oxide (rust) on its surface. Pack your bags; we're off to the rust bucket of the solar system.

> **ON JUPITER, THE STORMS ARE LARGER THAN** the entire Earth! The Great Red Spot, a storm that has been raging on Jupiter for at least 300 years, is so big that three Earths could fit inside it. Now that's a storm you don't want to get caught in.

> **EVER HEARD OF A MOON WITH ITS OWN** atmosphere? Titan, Saturn's largest Moon, boasts a thick atmosphere, even denser than Earth's! This mysterious Moon also has liquid methane lakes and rivers, giving scientists a reason to believe it could potentially support some form of life.

> **DID YOU KNOW THAT A DAY ON VENUS LASTS** longer than its year? Venus spins so slowly that it takes about 243 Earth days to complete one rotation, while it orbits the Sun in just 225 Earth days! Talk about taking your sweet time!

> **HERE'S A COSMIC** conundrum: Saturn is less dense than water! With an average density of 0.687 grams per cubic centimeter, Saturn would float if you could find a bathtub big enough to hold it.

> PICTURE ICE VOLCANOES ON PLUTO!

Recent data from the New Horizons spacecraft revealed that this icy dwarf planet might have cryovolcanoes, which erupt with a mixture of water, nitrogen, ammonia, and methane instead of molten lava. A frosty twist on a fiery phenomenon!

> IMAGINE A SOLAR ECLIPSE LASTING OVER

3 hours! On Jupiter, the moon Amalthea casts a shadow that can cause an eclipse lasting up to 3.5 hours!

> THE SUN'S MASS MAKES UP A STAGGERING

99.86% of the total mass of our solar system. Talk about hogging the cosmic limelight! Composed mostly of hydrogen and helium, the Sun is the ultimate powerhouse, providing us with all of the warmth and energy we need to survive.

EPIC SPACE EXPLORATION

> VIRGIN GALACTIC AND BLUE ORIGIN ARE

two companies making space tourism a reality for adventurous businesses and travelers. Soon, you might be able to book a ticket to visit space for a cosmic vacation. Pack your bags and get ready to walk the stairway to heaven!

> HAVE YOU HEARD OF THE DEEP SPACE

Gateway, the multi-purpose space station that will orbit the Moon? It is planned by NASA and is part of the grand plans of the Artemis program. It could serve as a destination on the pathway for future manned missions to Mars—and even beyond. The Deep Space Gateway could be an interplanetary pit-stop for weary space voyagers—like a cosmic Air B&B!

> COMPANIES LIKE PLANETARY RESOURCES,

inc., are developing technologies to develop asteroid mining, to obtain valuable resources like water, precious metals, and rare minerals. It's like an extraterrestrial gold rush! The race to tap into these celestial treasures is on, with companies involved in space ventures investment devising strategies as we speak!

> CAN YOU IMAGINE MUNCHING ON

space-grown salad? Since 2014, NASA scientists have been growing lettuce, wheat, and even zinnias aboard the international Space Station, making space farming a budding reality. Thanks to the Veggie Facility, a petite chamber designed for plant cultivation, astronauts are testing the possibility of growing their own food in space.

> EVER WONDERED WHAT IT TAKES TO

join the elite astronaut club? NASA's super-strict selection process involves swimming 75 meters in a bulky flight suit, treading water for 10 intense minutes, and acing a series of grueling physical and mental challenges such as sleep deprivation tests, solving complex problems while spinning in a giant centrifuge just to name a few.

> NAVIGATING THE LOO IN ZERO GRAVITY IS

no small feat for astronauts. On the international Space Station, the bathroom boasts a toilet equipped with foot straps and thigh bars to keep astronauts securely in place, because floating away mid-business is a definite no-go. They use a vacuum system to whoosh away waste into separate containers, turning a regular call of nature into a high-tech suction affair. Who knew space could complicate even the simplest of Earthly tasks?

> **DID YOU KNOW THAT FUTURE ASTRONAUTS** might be living on the Moon in the not-so-distant future? NASA's Artemis program, announced in 2019, aims to return humans to our lunar neighbor by 2026 and establish a sustainable human presence by 2028. This lunar base could serve as a launchpad for missions to Mars and beyond. Imagine stepping out of your front door to gaze at the Earthrise.

> **GRAB YOUR SHADES—SPACE IS ABOUT TO** get brighter! in 2019, a Russian startup called StartRocket revealed plans to launch a cluster of tiny satellites, creating artificial constellations called "orbital billboards." These cosmic ads would be visible from Earth, displaying messages and logos in the night sky. Not entirely sure how I feel about this one but I guess we'd have to say "Goodbye, shooting stars; hello, space commercials!"

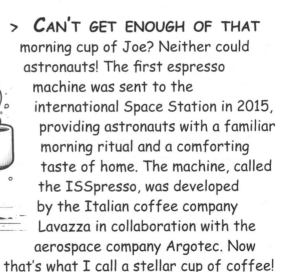

> **CAN'T GET ENOUGH OF THAT** morning cup of Joe? Neither could astronauts! The first espresso machine was sent to the international Space Station in 2015, providing astronauts with a familiar morning ritual and a comforting taste of home. The machine, called the ISSpresso, was developed by the Italian coffee company Lavazza in collaboration with the aerospace company Argotec. Now that's what I call a stellar cup of coffee!

INCREDIBLE FACTS FOR INQUISITIVE MINDS

> APOLLO 11 MADE HISTORY IN 1969

as NASA astronauts Neil Armstrong and Buzz
Aldrin became the first humans to walk on the Moon.
Remember Armstrong's famous words—"That's one small
step for man, one giant leap for mankind." Isn't it thrilling
to look up at the Moon at night and know that humans made
that landing more than 50 years ago?

> YOU MIGHT NOT KNOW THAT IN 2006

NASA's New Horizons mission launched an historic 9-year,
3-billion-mile journey to reach the icy dwarf planet
Pluto, revealing amazing details after it arrived in 2015.
The close encounter unveiled a treasure trove of planetary
features, such as vast plains, ice mountains, and even
perhaps an ocean underground that could be brewing life
beneath the icy surface.

> DID YOU KNOW THAT ASTRONAUTS ON THE

international Space Station (ISS) exercise at least two
hours each day to combat muscle and bone loss due to
microgravity. The sweat they produce evaporates and
is recycled, along with the water from their exhaled
breath, collected as condensation on the Space Station's
walls. The ISS water processing system uses these
water sources as drinkable water! It must take some iron
stomach to drink that!

> CAN YOU HEAR ME NOW? IN SPACE, NO ONE

can hear you scream—or anything else for that matter!
That's because sound waves need a medium to travel
through, and space is a vacuum. Turns out, the "sounds of
silence" really do exist!

> **DID YOU KNOW THAT IF YOU WERE AN**
astronaut on a spacewalk, your outfit would weigh around
280 pounds on Earth! This hefty space suit provides
life-supporting functions, shields against radiation, and
insulates astronauts from the temperature extremes of
space. So next time you complain about your winter coat
being too heavy, just be glad you're not gearing up for
a stroll in space!

> **EVER WONDERED HOW FAR HUMAN–MADE**
objects have traveled into space? Voyager 1, launched
by NASA in 1977, is currently over 14 billion miles away
from Earth. That's the like looping around Earth over
600,000 times! Its journey has been so long that it
takes over 22 hours for light itself to travel from the
spacecraft back to Earth.

> **IMAGINE SENDING A CAR TO SPACE!**
Elon Musk's SpaceX did just that in 2018 when they
launched a Tesla Roadster into space during the maiden
flight of the Falcon Heavy rocket. A mannequin named
"Starman" sat in the driver's seat, jamming to David
Bowie's "Space Oddity" on repeat. Talk about a road
trip to remember!

> **DURING THE 1970 APOLLO 13 MISSION,**
a catastrophic failure caused an oxygen tank to explode.
In the vacuum of space, the crew crafted a life-saving
hack using a plastic bag, cardboard, and duct tape,
transforming their space den fit only for into a "makeshift"
lifeboat for three. This quick thinking under pressure
ensured their safe return, marking the mission as
a testament to resourcefulness and calm in the face
of adversity.

> **How would you like to be the first**
tourist to circle the Moon? in 2026, SpaceX's Starship
plans to take Japanese billionaire Yusaku Maezawa and
a group of artists on a lunar adventure aboard the "Dear
Moon" project. This out-of-this-world trip is set to inspire
art that will truly be out of this world!

> **In 2021, SpaceX's inspiration4 mission**
made history as the first all-civilian crew to orbit Earth.
Led by billionaire Jared Isaacman, the crew included
a childhood cancer survivor, a science educator, and
a data engineer. They spent three days in space, raising
funds for St. Jude Children's Research Hospital while
enjoying the ultimate space adeventure!

> **In 2013, Italian astronaut**
Luca Parmitano's helmet started filling with water during
a spacewalk outside the ISS, due to a blockage in the
suit's cooling system. With quick thinking and teamwork,
Parmitano managed to return to the safety of the ISS.
That's one soggy spacewalk he'll
never forget!

> **Speaking of space**
oddities, did you know that
the Apollo 10 astronauts heard
strange music on the far side
of the Moon in 1969? The crew
was out of radio contact with
Earth when they picked up
eerie, whistling sounds on
their radio. Although likely
caused by radio interference,
it still makes for an intriguing
space mystery!

> **ARE YOU READY FOR EARTH-TO-EARTH**
travel on a rocket? SpaceX's Starship plans to
revolutionize transportation by using its reusable rocket
system for point-to-point travel on Earth. Imagine zipping
from New York to Sydney in just 30 minutes! Now that's
a speedy commute!

> **IMAGINE PLAYING GOLF ON THE MOON!**
in 1971, Apollo 14 astronaut
Alan Shepard did just that.
Using a custom 6-iron head
made that he could attach
to a lunar sampling tool,
Shepard took a swing
and sent two golf
balls soaring across
the lunar surface.
That's one small
swing for man,
one giant drive
for mankind!

> **DID YOU KNOW THAT ASTRONAUTS EAT ICE**
cream in space? Freeze-dried astronaut ice cream is
a popular snack aboard the ISS. While it may not have
the same creamy texture as the ice cream we enjoy
on Earth, it's still a sweet treat that satisfies those
space cravings!

> **IN 1969, DURING THE APOLLO 11 MISSION,**
Michael Collins captured a unique photograph featuring the
lunar module "Eagle" with Buzz Aldrin and Neil Armstrong
aboard, poised for their historic moon landing as well.

INCREDIBLE FACTS FOR INQUISITIVE MINDS

The remarkable thing about this image is that because Earth was also captured in the background it included every human alive at the time, except for Michael Collins. The photo has become aptly known as "Everyone in the world, except Michael Collins."

> ### DID YOU KNOW THAT PIZZA HAS BEEN
delivered to space? in 2001, Pizza Hut became the first company to send a pizza to the ISS for Russian cosmonaut Yuri Usachov. Although it cost a whopping $1 million, it certainly gives a new meaning to "out-of-this-world" delivery service!

> ### EVER THOUGHT OF SENDING A MESSAGE
in a bottle to space? NASA's Voyager 1 and 2 spacecraft, launched in 1977, carry "Golden Records" with sounds, images, and messages from Earth. These cosmic time capsules are meant for any intelligent extraterrestrial life that may find them, serving as an interstellar greeting from humanity.

> ### DID YOU KNOW
that astronaut Scott Kelly and his twin brother, Mark Kelly, were part of a groundbreaking study? Scott spent a year aboard the ISS while Mark remained on Earth. The "Twin Study" examined the effects of long-duration spaceflight on the human body, providing valuable insights for future missions to Mars and beyond.

> **IMAGINE WATCHING A MOVIE IN SPACE!**
in 2015, astronauts aboard the ISS enjoyed a special
screening of "The Martian," starring Matt Damon.
With Earth as their backdrop, it was a unique and fitting
way to unwind after a long day of space exploration.

> **READY FOR AN INTERPLANETARY ROAD TRIP?**
SpaceX's Starship, a fully reusable spacecraft, is
designed to transport up to 100 people to Mars and
other destinations in our solar system. With plans to
begin crewed missions as early as 2027, this incredible
feat of engineering may soon change the way we
explore space!

> **THE HUMAN-MADE OBJECT CURRENTLY**
furthest distance from Earth is the Voyager 1 spacecraft!
Launched in 1977, it's now an amazing 14 billion miles
(22 billion kilometers) away from our home planet, bearing
a Golden Record filled with images, music and sounds
representing humanity—like a message in a bottle. Talk
about a far-out mixtape!

> **CAN YOU PICTURE A BUSTLING MARTIAN CITY?**
SpaceX founder Elon Musk envisions a self-sustaining
Mars colony with a population of 1 million people by 2050.
To achieve this, he plans to send multiple Starships
carrying passengers, cargo, and supplies to the Red
Planet every 26 months, when Earth and Mars are closest
in their orbits.

> **AS THEY ORBIT EARTH AT A WHOPPING**
17,500 miles per hour (28,000 kilometers per hour),
astronauts aboard the international Space Station (ISS)
experience 16 sunrises and sunsets every 24 hours.
Talk about a time warp!

> **ON THE GEMINI 3 MISSION, ASTRONAUT**
John Young managed to sneak a corned beef sandwich into orbit, giving "fast food" a whole new altitude. This space snack, far from the freeze-dried fare approved by NASA, sparked both amusement and concern. Floating crumbs in zero-gravity posed a real risk to both astronauts and equipment, making this culinary contraband a memorable, if not exactly endorsed, part of space history.

> **IN A PERFORMANCE**
that's out of this world, astronaut Chris Hadfield became a cosmic rock star aboard the international Space Station (ISS) by covering David Bowie's "Space Oddity." His rendition, complete with a mesmerizing music video featuring the Earth as a backdrop, rocketed across social media, turning Hadfield into a viral sensation.

> **IN 1965, ON THE GEMINI 3 MISSION,**
astronaut John Young decided to spice up the space menu by smuggling a corned beef sandwich into orbit, courtesy of a Cocoa Beach deli. What seemed like a harmless prank quickly crumbled into a potential hazard, as NASA pointed out the danger of floating crumbs interfering with spacecraft equipment. This interstellar snack time became a legendary lesson in the importance of sticking to space-safe foods, proving that even in the vastness of the cosmos, it's the little things - or crumbs - that matter.

CHAPTER FOUR

AWESOME ANATOMY & MEDICAL MARVELS

AMAZING FACTS ABOUT OUR
BRILLIANT BODIES

> **CAN YOUR BONES ARE STRONGER THAN STEEL,** pound for pound! That's right! The human skeletal system has a strength-to-weight ratio that exceeds that of steel, making it incredibly sturdy and able to withstand immense pressure. If our skeleton were a superhero, it could support the weight of five hefty pickup trucks!

> **HAVE YOU EVER** considered how mighty your heart truly is? This phenomenal organ pumps enough blood throughout your lifetime to fill a whopping 3 million soda cans! It's working tirelessly to keep us nourished and full of energy every single day!

> **DON'T BLINK, OR YOU'LL MISS THIS** astonishing fact! We blink around 28,000 times a day on average, adding up to an incredible 10 million times per year. Our eyes are constantly working out, even when we don't realize it!

> **STICK YOUR TONGUE OUT FOR THIS FUN** fact: your tongue has its own unique identity! Just like fingerprints, no two tongue prints are the same. Time to consider adding tongue prints to your collection of selfies!

> YOUR BODY IS A NATURAL POWERHOUSE!
in just 30 minutes, the heat produced by your body is enough to boil half a gallon of water. Who needs an electric kettle when you've got such an incredible human body?

> READY FOR A HEIGHT-CHANGING REVELATION?
Throughout the day, gravity compresses our spines, making us shorter. But fear not! As we sleep, our spines decompress, and we regain our original height.

> THINK YOUR HAIR IS ONLY FOR TURNING
heads? If you were to create a rope using strands of your hair, it could support a mind-boggling weight of around 12 tons. Now that's what we call a hair-raising experience!

> SHOW SOME APPRECIATION FOR YOUR LIVER!
It's the only organ that can completely regenerate itself, even after losing up to 75% of its tissue. The liver is a true comeback king in the world of organs!

> CAN YOU SNIFF OUT THIS FACT? OUR NOSES
possess the incredible ability to remember up to 50,000 different scents. They're perfect for helping us identify that one mysterious smell lurking in the back of our fridges.

> BRACE YOURSELF FOR AN ASTOUNDING
intestinal journey! If you were to stretch out your small intestine, it would measure about 22 feet long, while your large intestine would span roughly 5 feet. Combined, they'd be longer than a blue whale! Now that's one impressive digestive highway!

> **EVER WONDERED WHY WE CAN'T HELP BUT** yawn when we see someone else do it? It's believed that yawning is a form of social bonding, enabling us to empathize with others and sync our moods. So go ahead and yawn away, guilt-free!

> **FEEL LIKE TICKLING YOURSELF? YOU MIGHT BE** disappointed! It's nearly impossible to tickle yourself because your brain anticipates the sensation, which means it doesn't produce the usual tickle response. Our brains truly are sneaky tricksters!

> **TAKE A DEEP BREATH AND DIVE INTO THIS** fact! While the average person can hold their breath for 30 seconds, some individuals, with proper training, can hold it for over 11 minutes. That's longer than most of your favorite pop songs!

> **HERE'S A FUN FACT THAT MIGHT LEAVE YOU** feeling a bit sweaty! Human sweat is actually odorless until it combines with bacteria on our skin. This mixture creates the infamous body odor we all know and (don't) love. Those pesky bacteria sure have a stinky side!

> **YOUR SKIN IS LIKE A STEALTHY CHAMELEON!** A single square inch of skin houses roughly 20 million microscopic cells that are constantly renewing themselves. It's like having a fresh start every single day!

> **GET READY FOR A SWIMMING REVELATION!** Babies are born with a natural instinct to hold their breath and kick their legs when submerged in water, making them tiny aquatic prodigies. Splish, splash, they're taking a bath!

> **ARE YOU A NIGHT OWL OR AN EARLY BIRD?**
Your preference for mornings or evenings may be genetically determined, so you can thank (or blame) your genes for those late-night Netflix binges or early morning jogs!

> **BRACE YOURSELF FOR THIS BOTANICAL**
bombshell: humans share about 60% of their DNA with... plants! That's right, we have more in common with our leafy friends than you might have thought.

> **YOUR BODY IS HOME TO AN ASTRONOMICAL**
number of bacteria! in fact, there are more bacteria living in your mouth right now than there are people on Earth. Talk about a party going on in there!

> **EVER WONDERED WHY PAPER CUTS HURT**
so much? It's because our fingers have a higher concentration of nerve endings, making them incredibly sensitive. Those sneaky paper cuts really know how to get us where it hurts!

> **DID YOU KNOW THAT**
your ears are constantly growing? As we age, the cartilage in our ears continues to grow, making them larger over time. We're all turning into Dumbo, one day at a time!

> **YOUR BRAIN IS**
a true energy guzzler! Despite making up only 2% of your body weight, it consumes a staggering 20% of your body's energy. Now that's a power-hungry organ!

> **Have you ever considered how many** taste buds you have? Your tongue is home to approximately 10,000 taste buds, and each of them is replaced every 10 to 14 days. Talk about a revolving door of flavor detectors!

> **If you've ever felt like you're shedding** hair like a dog, you're not far off! Humans lose around 50 to 100 hairs per day on average. It's no wonder we're constantly cleaning our brushes!

> **How's this for a nail-biting fact?** Fingernails grow about 3 to 4 times faster than toenails. So if you feel like you're always trimming your nails, now you know why!

> **Did you know that your stomach** produces a new layer of mucus every two weeks? It does this to prevent itself from being digested by its own powerful acids. That's some serious self-preservation!

> **Get ready for** a mind-blowing tear-jerker! Humans produce an average of 15 to 30 gallons of tears per year. That's enough to fill a small kiddie pool!

> **Who knew saliva could be** so impressive? The average person produces around 25,000 quarts of saliva in a lifetime, which is enough to fill two swimming pools. Better start practicing your backstroke!

> **STOMACH GROWLING AT YOU? THAT**
rumbling noise your stomach makes when it's empty is
called "borborygmi." It's caused by the movement of gas
and fluids through your digestive system. So, the next time
your tummy talks to you, you'll know what it's saying!

> **CAN YOU BELIEVE THAT YOUR BODY IS**
constantly producing new cells? in fact, it's estimated that
the human body creates about 25 million new cells every
second. It's like our own personal cellular factory!

> **ARE YOU AWARE THAT OUR EYES ARE ALWAYS**
the same size from birth? Despite our noses and ears
growing throughout our lives, our eyes remain constant.
Talk about being wide-eyed!

> **READY FOR A JAW-DROPPING FACT? HUMANS**
produce about 25,000 quarts of saliva in their lifetime,
enough to fill two swimming pools! Saliva plays a crucial role
in digestion, breaking down food, and keeping our mouths
healthy. Talk about a spit-tacular achievement!

> **THINK YOUR SKIN IS JUST A SIMPLE**
wrapper? Think again! Our skin is the largest organ
in our body, and it's responsible for protecting us from
harmful substances, regulating our body temperature, and
providing the sensation of touch. It's like our very own
superhero suit!

> **BRACE YOURSELF FOR AN EYE-OPENING**
revelation! The human eye can distinguish around 10 million
different colors. The eye's complex structure and
light-sensitive cells allow us to perceive the vibrant world
around us. No wonder they say beauty is in the eye of
the beholder!

> **DID YOU KNOW YOUR BODY IS**
a powerhouse? The energy generated by your muscles when
you're exercising is enough to boil half a gallon of water.
So, the next time you're breaking a sweat, just remember
you're a human kettle!

> **DID YOU KNOW YOUR BRAIN CAN GENERATE**
enough electricity to power a low-wattage LED light?
The brain's 100 billion neurons transmit and receive
electrical signals, producing a small amount of electricity.
It's no wonder they say knowledge is power!

> **GET READY TO BE TICKLED PINK! OUR BELLY**
buttons are home to thousands of bacteria, forming
a unique ecosystem called the "navel microbiome." Don't
worry, though - most of these bacteria are harmless and
even help maintain our overall health. Talk about a belly
full of surprises!

> **PREPARE FOR A HAIR-RAISING REVELATION!**
The average person has around 100,000 hair follicles on
their scalp. And surprisingly, blondes tend to have more
hair follicles than brunettes or redheads. Looks like
blondes have more than just fun!

> **DID YOU KNOW OUR EARS ARE ALWAYS**
working, even when we're asleep? Our brain can still
process sounds while snoozing, but it chooses to ignore
most of them. So, next time someone accuses you of not
listening, just tell them your brain was on a break!

> **HOLD YOUR BREATH FOR THIS ONE: OUR**
lungs are enormous! If you were to spread them out flat,
they'd cover an area about the size of a tennis court.
No wonder we can inhale up to 2,100 to 2,400 gallons of
air per day!

> Ready for a toe-tally amazing fact?

Our feet contain 26 bones, 33 joints, and over 100 muscles, tendons, and ligaments. With so many moving parts, it's no wonder they can support our entire body weight and keep us moving. Feet, we salute you!

> Feeling a little blue?

Blame your brain! The brain can't actually feel pain, despite being the organ that processes pain signals. This is why brain surgeries can sometimes be performed while the patient is awake. Talk about a mind-numbing experience!

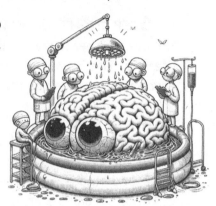

> Here's a nerve-wracking

fact: humans have around 45 miles of nerves running throughout their bodies. These nerves transmit information between our brains and the rest of our bodies at speeds of up to 250 miles per hour. Now that's a lightning-fast connection!

> Get ready to flex your trivia muscles:

humans have over 650 muscles in their bodies, accounting for around 40% of our total body weight. From blinking to walking, our muscles keep us moving and grooving all day long!

> Are you ready for a heartwarming fact?

Hugging releases oxytocin, a hormone that promotes feelings of love, bonding, and well-being. It's like a natural happy pill! So, go ahead and share a hug – it's good for you and those around you.

> **Can you stomach this fact? Your**
stomach acid is so strong that it can dissolve metal! Don't
worry, though, your stomach lining protects you from
digesting yourself. It's nature's way of keeping our insides
safe and sound.

> **Step right up for this fascinating fact:**
the average person will walk about 100,000 miles in their
lifetime. That's equivalent to walking around the Earth's
equator more than four times! Talk about a globetrotter!

> **Listen up for this ear-resistible fact:**
Your ears are made up of the smallest bones in your body,
called the ossicles. These three tiny bones – the malleus,
incus, and stapes – work together to transmit sound
vibrations from the eardrum to the inner ear. Talk about
a delicate dance of auditory awesomeness!

UNCONVENTIONAL MEDICAL TREATMENTS

> **Feeling a little under the weather?**
in the past, you might have been prescribed bloodletting!
This treatment, practiced well into the 19th century,
involved draining blood from patients to balance their
"humors" and restore health. Leeches or lancets were the
go-to tools for this procedure.

> **Fancy a trip to the dentist?**
Ancient Egyptians had a peculiar solution for toothaches:
dead mouse paste. They believed that applying mashed-up
dead mice to painful teeth would alleviate the pain,
making dental visits a bit more, well, interesting!

> IN 16TH-CENTURY FRANCE, A RENOWNED
surgeon named Ambroise Paré had a unique approach to
treating gunshot wounds. Instead of cauterizing them
with boiling oil, he applied a soothing mixture of egg
yolk, rose oil, and turpentine, which turned out to be
surprisingly effective.

> LOVE A GOOD SPA DAY? ROMANS BELIEVED
that gladiator sweat had healing properties. They
collected the sweat, mixed it with oils, and used it as
a skin ointment. Talk about a different kind of "glow up"!

> PLINY THE ELDER, A ROMAN NATURALIST,
had a bizarre cure for epilepsy. He recommended that
patients wear a necklace made of the foam produced by
a rabid dog's mouth. Not exactly a fashionable accessory,
but they believed it worked!

> FEELING A LITTLE BLUE? IN THE 18TH
century, doctors prescribed "laughing gas parties" to
combat depression. Nitrous oxide, or laughing gas, was
used as a recreational drug to lift patients' spirits.

> ARE YOU FAMILIAR WITH "CORPSE MEDICINE"?
in 17th-century Europe, physicians believed that consuming
powdered mummy remains could cure various ailments.
From headaches to stomach issues, mummies were
considered the go-to medicine for the time.

> IT'S NOT A SECRET THAT SMOKING IS BAD
for your health. But in the early 20th century, cigarettes
were marketed as a cure for asthma! Advertisements
claimed that inhaling tobacco smoke would open up the
airways and alleviate asthma symptoms.

> **EVER CONSIDERED SNAIL SLIME FOR A COUGH?** in the 18th century, snail syrup was a popular cough remedy. The concoction consisted of crushed snails, sugar, and several other weird and wonderful ingredients, was believed to soothe coughs and sore throats.

> **WHAT'S THE WEIRDEST THING YOU'VE PUT** in your eyes? in the 16th century, cataract treatment involved placing a drop of honey or a small, gold-plated needle directly on the eyeball. Ouch!

> **LOBOTOMY, ANYONE? IN THE MID-20TH** century, this controversial procedure involved severing connections in the brain's prefrontal cortex to treat mental disorders. Thankfully, this risky and often harmful practice has since been abandoned.

> **HAVE YOU EVER THOUGHT ABOUT** wearing a dead animal to ease your aches and pains? in the Middle Ages, doctors believed that strapping a live chicken or dead pigeon to swollen areas could help draw out harmful "vapors" causing the pain.

> **IN THE 19TH** century, tapeworm diet pills were all the rage. People believed that swallowing tapeworm cysts would lead to weight loss, as the parasitic worms would consume some of the ingested food in their host's intestines. While tapeworms might have led to some weight loss, they also

came with a host of unpleasant side effects, such as abdominal pain, diarrhea, and malnutrition. Definitely not the ideal diet plan!

> **CAN YOU IMAGINE A WORLD WHERE SNAILS** were a go-to remedy for an upset stomach? in ancient Rome, Pliny the Elder prescribed crushed snails as a remedy for indigestion. Patients in the 1st century AD would grind these slimy creatures into a paste and gulp it down, believing it would cure their ailments. Bon appétit, Rome!

> **HERE'S A CHILLING TALE FROM THE** 16th-century Europe: "corpse medicine" was all the rage! People believed that consuming human remains, particularly mummies, could cure various diseases. The macabre practice even involved the creation of "mummy powder," which was made from ground-up mummies imported from Egypt. Talk about an eerie elixir, Europe!

> **PICTURE THIS: 19TH-CENTURY ENGLAND AND** women are flocking to spas to soak in radioactive water! Madame Curie's discovery of radium in 1898 sparked a radioactive craze, leading people to believe that radium-infused water could rejuvenate the body and cure various ailments. Little did they know the dangers of radioactivity. Glowingly misguided, England!

> **FANCY A SWIG OF GOAT DUNG? IN MEDIEVAL** Europe, people suffering from the bubonic plague turned to a rather unpalatable treatment: a potion made from crushed emeralds and goat dung. They believed that this concoction would help cure the deadly disease. Unfortunately, the only thing it likely cured was their appetite. Cheers to that, medieval Europe!

> IN THE 18TH CENTURY, FRANCE WAS ABUZZ
with a shocking new therapy: "electric eel baths."
Patients suffering from various ailments would submerge
themselves in water filled with electric eels, believing
the shocks would cure their ills. Needless to say, this
electrifying experience left many patients feeling a bit
jolted. Quite the shocker, France!

> IN 19TH-CENTURY AMERICA, A PHYSICIAN
named Dr. John Harvey Kellogg believed that yogurt
enemas could cleanse the body and improve overall health.
Patients at his Battle Creek Sanitarium in Michigan
would receive this unconventional treatment, hoping
it would work wonders for their digestive systems.
Dairy daring, America!

> IN 18TH-CENTURY ENGLAND, PEOPLE BELIEVED
that eating a live frog could cure throat infections.
Patients would swallow a live frog whole, hoping that
the slippery amphibian would dislodge any troublesome
blockages in their throat. A real-life "frog in the throat"
moment, England!

> TOBACCO SMOKE ENEMAS WERE A REAL THING
in 18th-century Europe and America. This bizarre
treatment involved blowing tobacco smoke into a patient's
rectum to treat a variety of ailments, from headaches
to colds. It was even used as a resuscitation method for
drowning victims. Talk about a smoky situation, Europe
and America!

> IN ANCIENT EGYPT, AROUND 1500 BC,
crocodile dung was a popular contraceptive. Women
would mix the dung with honey and insert it into their
vaginas, believing that the concoction would prevent

pregnancy. We're not sure how effective this method was, but it definitely sounds like a croc(k) of... something, ancient Egypt!

> IN THE 16TH CENTURY, PARACELSUS,

a Swiss physician and alchemist, believed that drinking a concoction made from human skulls and alcohol could cure epilepsy. He would grind up pieces of skull and mix them with strong spirits to create his eerie elixir. Bottoms up, 16th-century Switzerland!

> IN 19TH-CENTURY AMERICA, A POPULAR

treatment for asthma involved inhaling the smoke from burning indian hemp, also known as cannabis. Patients would breathe in the smoke, believing it would help alleviate their asthma symptoms. High times for asthma sufferers, America!

> IN 16TH-CENTURY EUROPE,

it was believed that rubbing a bald man's head with fresh onions could cur warts. The onion juice was thought to have wart-removing properties, and the bald man's scalp was considered a good luck charm. A hair-raising treatment for sure, Europe!

> THE ANCIENT ROMANS

were known for their love of gladiator games, but did you know they also used gladiator sweat as a beauty treatment? Women would collect the sweat and dirt from a gladiator's body and use it as a face mask, believing it would make their skin look more youthful. Talk about a "glow up," ancient Rome!

> IN MEDIEVAL EUROPE, SOME PEOPLE BELIEVED that placing a live chicken on a swollen area of the body could help draw out the infection. They would pluck the chicken's feathers from its rear and apply it to the infected area, hoping the warmth and "energy" of the bird would heal them. A fowl remedy indeed, medieval Europe!

> DURING THE VICTORIAN ERA IN ENGLAND, it was believed that drinking a mixture of vinegar and chalk could help with indigestion. Patients would gulp down this unappetizing concoction, hoping it would ease their stomach troubles. A bitter pill to swallow, Victorian England!

> IN THE 18TH AND 19TH CENTURIES, SOME people believed that wearing a necklace made of earthworms could cure a sore throat. They would string together live earthworms and wear the necklace around their necks, hoping that the worms' natural secretions would soothe their ailment. Wriggly and weird, 18th and 19th-century Earth!

> ANCIENT EGYPTIANS BELIEVED THAT APPLYING a mixture of ground-up ostrich eggshells, dough, and incense to a broken bone could help it heal faster. This unusual plaster was thought to have magical properties that would speed up the healing process. A cracking good time, ancient Egypt!

> IN THE MIDDLE AGES, SOME PEOPLE BELIEVED that drinking a potion made from powdered human bones, moss from a skull, and blood from a decapitated head could cure epilepsy. This gory concoction was thought to contain powerful healing properties. Bloody bizarre, Middle Ages!

INCREDIBLE FACTS FOR INQUISITIVE MINDS

> IN 17TH-CENTURY FRANCE, A POPULAR treatment for syphilis involved ingesting mercury. Patients would take mercury pills or undergo mercury fumigation, believing that the toxic substance would kill the bacteria causing their illness. Unfortunately, the treatment often proved deadly, as mercury is highly toxic to humans. A heavy metal disaster, 17th-century France!

MEDICAL
BREAKTHROUGHS

> CAN YOU BELIEVE THAT A MOLDY PETRI DISH changed the course of modern medicine? in 1928, Scottish biologist Sir Alexander Fleming accidentally discovered penicillin, the world's first antibiotic. This breakthrough revolutionized medicine, saving countless lives by effectively treating bacterial infections. Talk about a happy accident!

> PICTURE THIS: A WORLD WITHOUT ORGAN transplants. Dr. Christiaan Barnard, a South African surgeon, changed the game in 1967 by performing the first successful human heart transplant. Barnard's groundbreaking surgery opened the door for life-saving organ transplant procedures worldwide. Hearts everywhere, rejoice!

> IMAGINE A WORLD WHERE PARALYZED patients regain their mobility! Swiss scientists led by Dr. Grégoire Courtine developed a revolutionary spinal implant

in 2018 that uses electrical stimulation to help paralyzed patients walk again. It's like a scene straight out of a sci-fi movie, but it's real life, and it's mind-blowing!

> ## PICTURE THIS: A "BIONIC

eye" that restores vision to the blind! Australian researchers at Bionic Vision Technologies developed the bionic eye in 2018, which uses a tiny camera to capture images and send electrical signals to the brain. This futuristic device has given hope to millions of people living with vision loss. Eye can't believe it!

> ## CAN YOU FATHOM GROWING

human organs in a lab? in 2013, scientists at the Wake Forest institute for Regenerative Medicine in North Carolina successfully grew a human ear using 3D printing and living cells. This groundbreaking research could revolutionize organ transplantation and give new hope to those in need. Ear-resistible work, indeed!

> ## WHAT IF WE COULD COMMUNICATE WITH OUR

brains alone? That's the vision behind Elon Musk's Neuralink, where they are developing a brain-machine interface for controlling computers, prosthetic limbs, and even enabling telepathic communication – all by using a chip implanted directly into the brain. And with the first successful demonstration allowing a paraplegic man to control all of his digital devices by mere thought, we can only expect things to get even more exciting. Now that's some next-level thinking!

> **EVER DREAMED OF ETERNAL YOUTH? RESEARCHERS** at the Salk institute in California made a groundbreaking discovery in 2016, demonstrating that they could partially reverse the aging process in mice by reprogramming their cells. This stunning finding could pave the way for revolutionary anti-aging treatments and bring us closer to the elusive fountain of youth. Age is just a number, after all!

> **GET READY FOR A TRIP TO THE CUTTING EDGE OF** medicine with 3D-printed organs! Pioneered by researchers like Dr. Anthony Atala, 3D bioprinting can create functional human organs using living cells as the "ink." This astonishing technology could potentially save millions of lives by providing tailor-made organs for transplantation. It's like something straight out of a sci-fi movie!

> **DR. HELEN TAUSSIG, A FEMALE CARDIOLOGIST** conceived a surgical technique that revived the hopes of those born with "blue baby syndrome," a life-threatening heart defect. The Blalock-Taussig-Thomas shunt, implemented first in 1944, saved over 900 children by the end of the 1940s and has since saved thousands more. Her ingenious insight pioneered modern pediatric cardiology earned her the title of a medical heroine.

> **AWARDED THE NOBEL PRIZE IN PHYSIOLOGY** or Medicine in 1988, Gertrude B. Elion developed drugs to treat leukemia, gout, herpes, and to prevent kidney transplant rejection. She didn't just create treatments; she crafted lifelines, saving countless lives with her medicinal mastery.

CHAPTER FIVE

AMAZING HUMAN FEATS & ATHLETIC ACHIEVEMENTS

UNUSUAL SPORTS FROM AROUND THE GLOBE

> **EVER HEARD OF WIFE CARRYING?** IN THE quaint town of Sonkajärvi, Finland, the Wife Carrying World Championships have been held annually since 1992. Husbands must carry their wives (or any woman weighing at least 49 kg) through a challenging obstacle course. The grand prize? The wife's weight in beer, of course!

> **CAN YOU IMAGINE PLAYING POLO ON AN** elephant? in 1982, two Brits in Nepal invented Elephant Polo, a slow-paced yet exhilarating sport. Elephant Polo Championships are held in various countries, with the World Elephant Polo Association overseeing the events. Talk about riding high on sportsmanship!

> **WHAT'S A SPORT THAT'LL SWEEP YOU OFF** your feet? Broomstick dancing! Originating in the 17th century in Lancashire, England, participants must dance and perform tricks with a broom, showcasing both agility and creativity. Who said cleaning couldn't be fun?

> **ARE YOU A FAN OF TAG? HOW ABOUT** "extreme" tag? World Chase Tag, founded in 2011 in the UK, is a professional sport where athletes chase and evade each other within a complex, obstacle-filled arena. High-speed parkour skills are essential for this adrenaline-pumping game!

INCREDIBLE FACTS FOR INQUISITIVE MINDS

> LOVE CHEESE? YOU'LL ADORE CHEESE

Rolling! Since the 19th century, people in Gloucester, England, have raced down a steep hill after a rolling wheel of cheese. The first to reach the bottom wins the cheese, along with a place in history! Picture a game of soccer, but with a twist - players are encased in giant inflatable bubbles! Welcome to Bubble Soccer, which started in Norway in 2011. It's a hilariously bouncy way to enjoy the beautiful game, with plenty of comical collisions!

> FANCY A GAME OF CHESS AND BOXING?

Chessboxing, created in 2003 in Berlin, Germany, alternates between rounds of chess and boxing. Competitors must be quick with their fists and their minds, as a checkmate or knockout can win the match!.

> CAN YOU BALANCE ON

a slackline? How about playing tennis on it? Slackline Tennis, originating in the Czech Republic in 2010, pushes the limits of balance and coordination. Players volley a ball back and forth while precariously perched on a slackline. Talk about a high-wire act!

> EVER PLAYED VOLLEYBALL

with your feet? Sepak Takraw, an ancient sport from Southeast Asia, has players using their feet, knees, and heads to keep a rattan ball in the air. With gravity-defying kicks and flips, it's an acrobatic spectacle like no other!

> **FANCY YOURSELF A LUMBERJACK? LOGROLLING,** a sport with roots in 19th-century North American logging camps, requires two competitors to balance on a floating log. The objective? Spin the log to make your opponent lose their footing and fall into the water!

> **IS SOCCER TOO EASY FOR YOU? HOW ABOUT playing it on** stilts? Stilt soccer, popular in West African countries like Nigeria and Burkina Faso, takes the beautiful game to new heights. With impressive balance and skill, players kick, pass, and score while towering above the field!

> **THE BIZARRE ORIGIN OF THE HIGH-FIVE dates back to** 1977 during a baseball game between the Los Angeles Dodgers and the Houston Astros. Dodgers outfielder Dusty Baker hit a home run, and as he jogged to home plate, his teammate Glenn Burke raised his hand high above his head. Baker, not knowing what to do, slapped it - and just like that, the high-five was born. Baseball fans everywhere, you're welcome!

ICONIC ATHLETES & THEIR ACHIEVEMENTS

> **CAN YOU IMAGINE WINNING 22 OLYMPIC** medals? American swimmer Michael Phelps, nicknamed the "Flying Fish," dominated the pool between 2004 and 2016. With a total of 28 medals (23 gold!), he's the most decorated Olympian of all time. With size 14 feet acting like flippers, it's no wonder he swam his way to legendary status!

> **FLOAT LIKE A BUTTERFLY, STING LIKE A BEE!**
Boxing legend Muhammad Ali, born Cassius Clay, was known
for his lightning-fast footwork and devastating punches.
A three-time world heavyweight champion, Ali was also
a social activist and a cultural icon. His poetic trash-talking
and unwavering confidence made him "The Greatest."

> **MEET THE "QUEEN OF THE COURT":**
Serena Williams! Since her professional debut in 1995,
she's won 23 Grand Slam singles titles and four Olympic
gold medals. Serena's powerful serve, fierce determination,
and unyielding work ethic make her a tennis legend.
Fun fact: She won the 2017 Australian Open while two
months pregnant!

> **WHO NEEDS A CAPE WHEN YOU CAN**
dominate the basketball court? in 1984, the high-flying
Michael Jordan made his NBA debut for the Chicago
Bulls, and the rest is history! Jordan, also known as "His
Airness," won 6 NBA championships and 5 MVP awards
throughout his legendary career.

> **WHAT'S MORE INTIMIDATING THAN FACING**
Mike Tyson in the boxing ring? in 1986, at just 20 years
old, Tyson became the youngest heavyweight boxing
champion, earning him the moniker "Iron Mike." With
44 knockouts under his belt, Tyson's opponents were left
quaking in their boots!

> **TOM BRADY, AN AMERICAN FOOTBALL**
quarterback, defied age and expectations by winning his
seventh Super Bowl in 2021 at the age of 43. Not only did
he secure a win for the Tampa Bay Buccaneers, but he also
snagged the Super Bowl MVP title!

> **CAN YOU BELIEVE THE FASTEST MAN ALIVE**
was almost late? in Beijing, 2008, Usain Bolt, the Jamaican
sprinter, nearly missed his chance to make history. Bolt
slept through his alarm, barely making it to the stadium,
but still managed to set a world record in the 100-meter
race, running at a mind-boggling 9.69 seconds!

> **IN 2000, VINCE CARTER, AN**
American basketball player,
leaped to stardom during
the Olympics in Sydney,
Australia. During a game
against France, he jumped
over 7-foot-2-inch
tall French center
Frédéric Weis.
Carter's incredible
dunk earned him the
nickname "Half-Man,
Half-Amazing."

> **WOULD YOU**
believe a 12-year-old
could serve a tennis ball faster than a cheetah can run?
in 1993, Venus Williams, at just 12 years old, served
a tennis ball at a mind-blowing 100 miles per hour. That's
faster than a cheetah's top speed! Williams went on to
become one of the most successful tennis players of
all time.

> **IN 1999, AMERICAN SKATEBOARDER**
Tony Hawk landed the first-ever 900-degree
spin in skateboarding history during the X Games in San
Francisco. The 900, which involves spinning two and a half
times in mid-air, propelled Hawk into the pantheon of
extreme sports legends

> IN 2017, ALEX HONNOLD, AN AMERICAN rock climber, ascended the 3,000-foot vertical granite wall of El Capitan in Yosemite National Park, California – all without ropes or safety gear. Honnold's death-defying feat, known as "free solo" climbing, took him a hair-raising 3 hours and 56 minutes to complete.

> WHO'S SCORED MORE GOALS FOR A SINGLE club than any other player in history? That's right, it's Argentina's Lionel Messi, who netted a mind-boggling 672 goals for FC Barcelona between 2004 and 2021. Talk about a one-club wonder!

> WHO'S THE ONLY PLAYER TO HAVE SCORED 100 points in a single NBA game? That would be the towering Wilt "The Stilt" Chamberlain, who achieved this colossal feat while playing for the Philadelphia Warriors in 1962. Score!

> REMEMBER WHEN BABE RUTH, THE "SULTAN of Swat," hit a jaw-dropping 714 home runs during his illustrious baseball career? This legendary slugger played for the Boston Red Sox, New York Yankees, and the Boston Braves between 1914 and 1935, making history with each swing.

> HOW MANY SUPER BOWL RINGS CAN ONE quarterback have? For Tom Brady, that number is a staggering 7! This gridiron great has been calling the shots since 2000 and shows no signs of slowing down, making him the G.O.A.T. of the NFL.

> ARE YOU READY TO RIDE THE WAVE OF trivia with the king of surf, Kelly Slater? This American surfing legend has won an unbelievable 11 World Surf League Championships and is the youngest (at 20) and oldest (at 39) surfer to win a title.

> **CRISTIANO RONALDO, THE MADEIRA,**
Portugal sensation, has been making jaws drop since
2002. With over 800 career goals, he's not just a goal
machine but a philanthropist too! Remember when he sold
his 2013 Ballon d'Or trophy and donated the proceeds to
a children's hospital? Ronaldo's off-the-chart skills and
golden heart make him the ultimate soccer icon.

> **ROGER FEDERER, THE SWISS MAESTRO, HAS**
been enchanting fans since 1998. His 237 consecutive
weeks as world No.1 still stands unmatched! Federer once
played an epic 4 hour and 48-minute Wimbledon final
against Rafael Nadal in 2008. His grace under pressure and
artistic strokes prove he's tennis royalty.

> **READY TO TAKE A HIGH-SPEED JOURNEY WITH**
the legend who revolutionized Formula 1 racing? Michael
Schumacher, the German speed demon, raced into the
history books in 1991. With 91 Grand Prix wins, this champ
was unstoppable! Did you know he once climbed from 16th
to 2nd place in just 20 laps at the 1995 Belgian Grand
Prix? Schumacher's fearlessness and sheer determination
make him a true racing icon.

> **HOW MANY HOCKEY PLAYERS DO YOU KNOW**
who've scored over 200 points in a single season? Wayne
Gretzky, "The Great One" from Brantford, Ontario, has
been leaving fans breathless since 1978. He accomplished
the 200-point feat four times! One memorable moment was
his 1981 game against the St. Louis Blues, scoring five goals
in a single game. Gretzky's extraordinary vision and skill
have solidified his legendary status.

> **WHO'S THE BASKETBALL LUMINARY WHO ONCE**
outscored an entire opposing team for three-quarters of
a game? Kobe Bryant, Philadelphia's pride, took the NBA by

storm in 1996. With five NBA championships under his belt, Kobe's incredible 81-point game in 2006 showcased his unwavering drive. His dedication to mastering his craft has made him one of the all-time greats.

> **EVER SEEN AN MMA FIGHTER SO VERSATILE,** he dominates in two weight divisions? Georges St-Pierre, Quebec's martial arts maestro, has been a force to reckon with since 2002. This UFC legend reclaimed his Middleweight title after a four-year hiatus! GSP's epic comeback victory over Michael Bisping in 2017 is a testament to his adaptability and fighting spirit.

> **CAN YOU FATHOM A BOXER WITH A PERFECT** 50-0 professional record? Floyd Mayweather Jr., Grand Rapids' undefeated prodigy, has been delivering knockout performances since 1996. His 2017 fight against Conor McGregor, which grossed over $550 million, showcased his impenetrable defense. Mayweather's tactical brilliance and incredible agility have cemented his place among boxing's all-time greats.

UNUSUAL HABITS OF
WORLD-CLASS ATHLETES

> **WHO KNEW THAT THE WORLD'S FASTEST MAN** had a love affair with... chicken nuggets? During the 2008 Beijing Olympics, Jamaican sprinter Usain Bolt devoured 1,000 chicken nuggets over the course of ten days, averaging a whopping 100 nuggets per day! Bolt claimed it was because he wasn't a fan of Chinese food and found solace in the familiar taste of nuggets.

> **CAN YOU IMAGINE A BASKETBALL LEGEND**
with a quirky pregame ritual involving a gooey, nutty treat?
Michael Jordan, the iconic NBA star, had a peculiar habit
of eating a peanut butter and jelly sandwich before every
game. His highness believed this sweet and sticky combo
kept him energized and ready to dominate the court.

> **EVER THOUGHT PROFESSIONAL SOCCER PLAYERS**
would turn to hair gel for good luck? Portuguese soccer
sensation Cristiano Ronaldo once admitted that his peculiar
hair gel ritual before each match brought him good
fortune. He would apply precisely the same amount of hair
gel to maintain his perfectly styled hair and,
hopefully, ensure a victory on the field.

> **WHAT'S THE CONNECTION**
between tennis and freezing cold
showers? Spanish tennis champion
Rafael Nadal would take icy cold
showers before each match, believing
it helped him get in the right frame
of mind to tackle his opponents.
Talk about shocking your system
into action!

> **WHAT DO GOLFERS AND**
bubble gum have in common?
American golfer Tiger Woods made it a point to chew
gum while playing, especially during critical moments. He
believed it helped him maintain focus and reduce stress, all
while keeping his breath minty fresh!

> **WHO WOULD'VE THOUGHT THAT THE NFL**
would have a player known as "Captain Underpants"?
Peyton Manning, one of the greatest quarterbacks

in history, wore the same pair of lucky underwear for every game during his rookie season. While it may not have been the most hygienic choice, it seemed to work wonders for his game!

> **IMAGINE A PROFESSIONAL SWIMMER REFUSING** to wash his hair during competitions! American swimming legend Michael Phelps had an odd habit of avoiding shampoo and hair washing during major tournaments. He believed his unwashed hair brought him good luck, and with 28 Olympic medals to his name, who are we to argue?

> **WHO WOULD HAVE THOUGHT A LEGENDARY** soccer player would talk to his legs for motivation? Zlatan Ibrahimovic, the charismatic Swedish soccer star, was known to have conversations with his legs before each game. He believed that by talking to them, they would listen and perform better during the match.

> **PICTURE A STAR BASEBALL PLAYER WITH AN** unusual chewing habit! New York Yankees slugger Babe Ruth was known to chew on a wad of licorice during games. The Great Bambino believed this sticky, sweet treat kept his mouth moist and helped him focus on hitting those iconic home runs.

> **TOM BRADY HAD A HABIT OF EATING EXACTLY** three chocolate chip cookies before every game. The legendary New England Patriots star believed these sweet treats provided him with a quick energy boost and a taste of home.

> **FLOYD MAYWEATHER JR., THE PUGILISTIC** prodigy from Grand Rapids, is notorious for abstaining from sex for months before his high-stakes fights. This

quirky practice might just be the secret sauce that keeps Mayweather's focus razor-sharp! Perhaps it's true what they say: abstinence makes the heart punch harder.

ATHLETIC ABSURDITIES & GAME DAY DRAMAS

> **REMEMBER WHEN MIKE TYSON TURNED** a boxing match into a chew-out session? During their heated 1997 rematch, Tyson infamously bit off a piece of Evander Holyfield's ear. This bizarre moment not only cost Tyson $3 million in fines but also resulted in a year-long ban from boxing, sparking lawsuits and leaving a permanent mark on his once-stellar reputation. The bite effectively turned a moment of impulse into an enduring legacy of infamy.

> **TALK ABOUT A WILD PITCH! IN A 2001 MLB** spring training game, Randy Johnson threw a fastball that fatefully collided with a bird in mid-flight. The feathered interloper exploded in a puff of feathers, marking one of baseball's most unexpected and feathery interruptions.

> **IN THE 1986 WORLD CUP, DIEGO** Maradona pulled off an undercover maneuver, known as the "Hand of God" goal. With a sneaky sleight of hand, he nudged the ball mid-air into England's net, and shockingly, the referee missed the incident completely. This divine intervention (or crafty cheat) gifted Argentina a crucial goal, paving their way to a 2-1 victory and eventual World Cup win.

INCREDIBLE FACTS FOR INQUISITIVE MINDS

> **EVER HAD AN**
unexpected guest drop
in? That's exactly what
happened during the
Bowe-Holyfield II fight
in 1993, when a man
dubbed 'Fan Man'
dramatically paraglided
right into the boxing
ring! His unscripted
cameo caused quite the
stir, halting the match and creating
a spectacle that was more circus than boxing.

> **BACK IN 1993, DURING HIS ROOKIE SEASON**
with the Orlando Magic, Shaquille O'Neal brought a whole
new meaning to "bringing down the house." in a game
against the New Jersey Nets, Shaq dunked so ferociously
that he not only broke the backboard but also brought
down the entire support structure! The game was delayed
for over half an hour as the bewildered crew scrambled to
set up a replacement hoop.

> **IN 1993, A CHILLING INCIDENT OCCURRED**
when Monica Seles was stabbed by a deranged fan
during a Women's Tennis Association quarterfinal match
in Hamburg, Germany. The attacker, motivated by his
fanatic support for opponent, Steffi Graf, aimed to disrupt
Seles' promising performance. This shocking underscored
the alarming vulnerabilities athletes face, even in highly
secured environments

> **DURING A 2012 NHL GAME, A SHOT BY**
Philadelphia Flyers' player Chris Pronger vanished into
thin air—or so it seemed. The puck actually lodged itself

in the goalie's skate, unnoticed for several minutes while gameplay continued. It was only discovered during a stoppage, providing a few chuckles and a lot of puzzled looks.

> At THE PLAYERS Championship

in 1998, Brad Fabel's play on the 17th hole took a bizarre turn when a seagull swooped down, and—after a few attempts—picked up the ball from the green and flew off, only to drop it into the water hazard! Luckily, the rules allowed him to replace the ball without penalty. It's not every day you see a bird so literally involved in a game of birdies!

AMAZING FEATS: PUSHING THE BODY TO THE EXTREME!

> Ready to meet the real-life Iceman?

Wim Hof, hailing from the Netherlands, defied the freezing cold in 2011 by immersing himself in ice for a teeth-chattering 1 hour, 52 minutes, and 42 seconds! But that's not the only cool trick up his sleeve. This chilly champ also dared to climb Mount Everest, and get this, without a top on! Talk about not sweating the small stuff—or the cold, for that matter.

> Budimir Šobat from Croatia, armed

with nothing but a lungful of air (and a sneaky trick up his sleeve involving hyperoxygenation), held his breath underwater for a jaw-dropping 24 minutes and 33 seconds in 2021. Yes, you read that right! This underwater wizard used a bit of science to turn his lungs into oxygen tanks, making fish everywhere question their life choices.

> **THEY SAY SLOW AND STEADY WINS THE** race, but how about running 350 miles non-stop? Meet Dean Karnazes, the American ultramarathon runner who, in 2005, pushed his body to the extreme and completed this jaw-dropping distance in 80 hours and 44 minutes! Talk about a running machine!

> **CAN YOU IMAGINE HOW MANY PUSH-UPS ONE** can do in a day? in 1989, Paddy Doyle from the UK managed to pump out an astounding 1,500,230 push-ups in a single year! That's like doing push-ups from London to Paris!

> **EVER TRIED THE PLANK EXERCISE?** It's tough, right? Well, not for George Hood from the USA, who in 2020, held a plank for an awe-inspiring 8 hours, 15 minutes, and 15 seconds! That's enough time to binge-watch your favorite series!

> **HOW MANY HULA HOOPS CAN YOU SPIN AT** once? If you thought five was impressive, think again! in 2019, Marawa Ibrahim from Australia spun a staggering 200 hula hoops simultaneously! Talk about being in a spin frenzy!

> **IN THE REALM OF JAW-DROPPING FEATS,** Randy Gardner's 1965 record of staying awake for 11 days and 24 minutes was a blink-and-you'll-miss-it moment in history. Yet, before you reach for a caffeine boost in homage, consider this: Robert McDonald went even further in 1986, pushing past the boundaries of sleeplessness to a staggering 18 days, 21 hours, and

40 minutes. This record-setting vigil not only surpassed Gardner's mark but also led Guinness World Records to retire the category, deeming the risk of such extreme sleep deprivation too perilous for future challengers.

> **HAVE YOU EVER TRIED TO TEAR A PHONEBOOK** in half? in 2007, Edward Charon from the USA ripped through 13 phonebooks, each with over 1,000 pages, in just one minute! Hello, Mr. Incredible!

> **REMEMBER WHEN YOU** used to try walking on your hands as a kid? Well, in 1990, Ashrita Furman from the USA took it up a notch by hand-walking a dizzying 3.2 miles in New York City! Talk about turning the world upside down!

> **HAVE YOU EVER TRIED** to fit yourself into a small space? in 2014, Leslie Tipton from the USA squeezed herself into a box measuring just 20.04 inches on each side! That's tighter than a can of sardines!

> **IMAGINE SKIPPING AS FAST AS YOU CAN.** In 2005, Ayumi Sakamaki from Japan managed to complete an incredible 162 skips in just 30 seconds! That's more skips than a kangaroo on a sugar rush!

> **CAN YOU IMAGINE STAYING UNDERWATER FOR** days on end? in 2015, Cem Karabay from Turkey spent an unbelievable 192 hours and 19 minutes underwater with scubagear, setting a new world record! That's like living in Atlantis!

> **CAN YOU BALANCE ON ONE FOOT FOR A LONG** time? in 1997, Suresh Joachim from Sri Lanka balanced on one foot for an astonishing 76 hours and 40 minutes! That's longer than most TV show marathons!

> **IN 2010, LEWIS PUGH FROM THE UK SWAM** one kilometer in the Arctic Ocean's icy waters, where temperatures plunged below 28°F! Lewis challenged the limits of human physiology, enduring hypothermia and frostbite. Brrr-illiant, wouldn't you say?

> **ARE YOU AFRAID OF HEIGHTS? IN 2012,** Felix Baumgartner from Austria free-fell from a stratospheric altitude of 128,100 feet, not only breaking the sound barrier but also exposing his body to near-vacuum conditions and extreme temperatures. He defied the odds, proving the human body could withstand such extreme conditions!

> **EVER HEARD OF SOMEONE RUNNING** 50 marathons in 50 days? in 2006, Dean Karnazes from the USA accomplished this jaw-dropping feat across 50 US states, pushing his body to unimaginable levels of endurance! No pain, no gain, right?

> **IMAGINE STAYING IN A SAUNA HEATED TO** a scorching 230°F! in 2003, Timo Kaukonen from Finland endured this blistering heat for 5 minutes and 14 seconds during the Sauna World Championships. However, in 2010, the competition took a grim turn. Timo was defending his title when tragedy struck, leading to the unfortunate passing of his Russian rival, Vladimir Ladyzhenskiy, after they both endured extreme conditions. This harrowing event led to the permanent cancellation of the championships, closing a chapter on this fiery test of human endurance.

> **HOW MANY HOURS CAN YOU DANCE WITHOUT**
stopping? in 2010, Kalamandalam Hemlata from
india performed a classical indian dance for a breathtaking
123 hours and 15 minutes straight, pushing her
body's limits to the extreme! Now that's dancing like
nobody's watching!

> **CAN YOU IMAGINE RUNNING UP A VERTICAL**
wall without any ropes? in 2012, Dan Goodwin from the
USA, also known as "Spider-Dan," scaled the 1,099-foot
Willis Tower in Chicago using only suction cups and
a Spider-Man suit! This gravity-defying achievement
proved humans could conquer even the tallest of
skyscrapers!

> **CAN YOU WRAP YOUR HEAD AROUND THE**
idea of tightrope walking across the Grand Canyon?
in 2013, daredevil Nik Wallenda from the USA performed
this heart-stopping feat on a 2-inch-wide steel cable
suspended 1,500 feet above the canyon floor! With no
safety harness, Nik relied solely on his incredible balance
and nerves of steel, proving that humans can achieve the
seemingly impossible!

> **HAVE YOU EVER HEARD OF SOMEONE CYCLING**
the entire length of Africa? in 2015, Mark Beaumont
from Scotland embarked on a 6,750-mile journey
from Cairo to Cape Town, pushing his body through
scorching deserts, treacherous mountain passes, and
the ever-changing African landscape. Mark completed
this epic adventure in just 42 days, setting a new
world record and demonstrating the immense power
of human determination!

> HOW ABOUT ENDURING THE MOST
bone-chilling cold while swimming? in 2002, Lynne Cox
from the USA swam 1.2 miles across the freezing waters
of the Antarctic, where the water temperature was a mere
32°F! Lynne's remarkable swim showcased the incredible
resilience of the human body, proving that even the iciest
waters can't freeze our spirit!

> HAVE YOU EVER THOUGHT OF SOMEONE
surviving a free fall from an airplane without
a parachute? in 1972, Vesna Vulović, a Serbian flight
attendant, miraculously survived a 33,330-foot plunge
after her plane exploded mid-air. Defying all odds and
medical expectations, Vesna not only lived through this
mind-boggling ordeal but also became a symbol of human
resilience and survival!

CHAPTER SIX

THE WACKY WORLD OF FILM & POP CULTURE

ICONIC FILMS & SHOWS

> DID YOU KNOW THAT FOR THE FILMING OF
"Batman Returns," a staggering $2 million was spent just
to ensure real penguins could be used on set? This budget
covered cooling, food, accommodation, and shipping for the
feathered actors, showcasing the lengths filmmakers will
go to authentically depict the Penguin's arctic world.

> DID YOU KNOW THAT THE "STAR WARS"
character Chewbacca was inspired by George Lucas's dog,
an Alaskan Malamute named indiana? The furry sidekick
became a beloved part of the franchise, making Wookiee
sounds and all. Who's a good co-pilot?

> EVER WONDERED HOW THEY FILMED THE
floating pen scene in "2001: A Space Odyssey"? The pen
was actually stuck to a sheet of glass that was rotated to
make it appear as if it was floating in zero gravity. Now
that's a creative solution to defy gravity!

> CAN YOU BELIEVE THAT THE ICONIC LINE
"Here's Johnny!" from the 1980 film "The Shining" was
improvised by Jack Nicholson? The actor drew inspiration
from the popular catchphrase of late-night talk show host
Johnny Carson. Now that's a smashing bit of trivia!

> THE EERIE SHARK FROM "JAWS" HAD
a nickname on set – Bruce! Named after Steven Spielberg's
lawyer, the mechanical shark often malfunctioned, causing
filming delays. But it all worked out in the end, as the
movie became a classic, making everyone afraid to go
in the water.

INCREDIBLE FACTS FOR INQUISITIVE MINDS

> IN THE **TV** SERIES "BREAKING BAD,"
the character Walter White's iconic blue meth was
actually made of rock candy. The show's creators chose
the vibrant blue color to make the illegal substance stand
out on screen. Sweet and sinister at the same time!

> DID YOU KNOW THAT THE
famous spaghetti scene in "Lady
and the Tramp" wasn't part of the
original script? Animator Frank
Thomas created the charming
scene to show the growing
connection between the two
characters. The result? One of
the most romantic moments
in Disney history!

> FOR THE MOVIE "FORREST GUMP,"
Tom Hanks wasn't initially paid for his role. Instead, he
took a percentage of the film's earnings, which turned
out to be a wise decision as the movie became a massive
box office hit. Life is like a box of chocolates, indeed!

> IN "THE GODFATHER," THE INFAMOUS HORSE
head scene used a real horse's head. It was acquired
from a dog food company that processed dead
animals. The shocking scene, which was meant to send
a powerful message, became one of the film's most
memorable moments.

> THE POPULAR **TV** SHOW "FRIENDS"
originally had a different title. The creators initially called
it "insomnia Cafe" before settling on the title we know and
love today. Could it BE any more iconic?

> IN THE MOVIE **"TITANIC,"** THE SCENE WHERE
Jack teaches Rose how to spit was improvised by Leonardo
DiCaprio and Kate Winslet. Director James Cameron liked
the playful moment so much that he decided to keep it
in the film. Ah, the magic of spontaneous creativity!

> **THE FAMOUS DELOREAN TIME MACHINE**
in "Back to the Future" was almost a refrigerator!
The filmmakers changed it to a car due to concerns that
children might imitate the film and get trapped in fridges.
Great Scott, what a close call!

> IN **"JURASSIC PARK,"**
to create the T-Rex's roar, sound
designer Gary Rydstrom combined the
sounds of a baby elephant, a tiger,
and an alligator. The result was the
bone-chilling, spine-tingling sound
that made the T-Rex one of the most
terrifying movie monsters ever.

> **DID YOU KNOW THAT**
during the filming of "The Wizard of
Oz," the dog that played Toto earned
more money than most of the human actors? Toto's salary
was $125 a week, while the Munchkins only made $50. No
place like home for this pampered pooch!

> **THE TERRIFYING SHOWER SCENE IN ALFRED**
Hitchcock's "Psycho" took seven days to shoot and used
over 70 camera angles. The final result is a masterful,
suspenseful sequence that made viewers think twice about
stepping into the shower.

INCREDIBLE FACTS FOR INQUISITIVE MINDS

> IN "E.T. THE EXTRA-TERRESTRIAL,"
the young Drew Barrymore didn't know that E.T. was an animatronic puppet. Director Steven Spielberg wanted to capture her genuine reactions, so he told her that E.T. was a real alien. Now that's some method acting!

> THE ICONIC "I'LL BE BACK" LINE FROM
"The Terminator" was originally scripted as "I'll come back." Arnold Schwarzenegger suggested the change to make the line sound more natural with his Austrian accent. The result? A catchphrase for the ages!

> DURING THE FILMING OF "CAST AWAY,"
production was halted for a year so that Tom Hanks could lose weight and grow his beard for the later scenes. The dedication paid off, as Hanks delivered a powerful and memorable performance in the film.

> DID YOU KNOW THAT "THE SIMPSONS"
creator Matt Groening named the show's characters after his own family members? Homer, Marge, Lisa, and Maggie are all named after Groening's relatives, while Bart is an anagram for "brat." That's one way to immortalize your family!

> CONTINUING WITH "THE SIMPSONS,"
can you believe that it is the longest-running American sitcom, making us laugh since 1989? With over 700 episodes, it holds the record for the longest-running primetime scripted TV show in history!

> DO YOU KNOW HOW MANY SWORDS WERE
used in the iconic Iron Throne from "Game of Thrones"? It was constructed using a whopping 200 swords!

This fantasy mega-hit had viewers on the edge of their seats from 2011 to 2019, with its epic battles and jaw-dropping plot twists.

> **DID YOU KNOW THAT THE ACTOR WHO PLAYED** Gunther, the lovable barista on "Friends," only got the role because he could operate an espresso machine? Talk about the perfect blend of skill and opportunity!

> **DID YOU KNOW THAT "SEINFELD," THE SHOW** about nothing, was nearly cancelled after its first season? It went on to become one of the most beloved sitcoms of all time, airing from 1989 to 1998 and leaving a legacy of timeless catchphrases.

> **IN THE CLASSIC SCI-FI SERIES "STAR TREK,"** the phrase "Beam me up, Scotty" was never actually uttered by Captain Kirk. This misquote has become a cultural phenomenon, proving that sometimes, the truth is stranger than fiction!

> **DID YOU KNOW THAT THE FAMOUS** "That's what she said" joke from "The Office" almost didn't make the cut? The show's producers were initially worried that the risqué punchline would be too offensive for TV. However, they ultimately decided to include it, and it became one of the show's most iconic catchphrases, solidifying Michael Scott's status as the king of awkward humor.

> **WHAT'S THE MOST UNLIKELY FILM TO INSPIRE** a fashion trend? The 1998 Coen Brothers' film "The Big Lebowski" sparked a resurgence in bowling shirt popularity. Dude, that's one fashionable flick!

STYLES, TRENDS, AND FASHION STATEMENTS!

> **REMEMBER THAT ICONIC MEAT DRESS?**
Lady Gaga's legendary outfit from the 2010 MTV Video Music Awards was made from real meat, and the designer, Franc Fernandez, later revealed that the ensemble smelled quite fresh during the event. Talk about a raw fashion statement!

> **LOVE THEM OR HATE THEM,**
crocs have a fascinating origin story. Originally created as slip-resistant boating shoes in 2002, these foam clogs quickly gained a polarizing reputation. Yet, they've sold over 300 million pairs and have strutted down high-fashion runways, proving that even the most controversial footwear can find success.

> **CAN YOU IMAGINE A DRESS THAT'S MADE FROM**
the same material as your favorite childhood toy? in 2011, a LA-based designer created a dress made entirely of LEGO bricks for singer, Fergie. A total of 20,000 colorful pieces were used to create this playful masterpiece!

> **CAN YOU IMAGINE A WORLD WHERE MICHAEL**
Jackson wasn't the King of Pop? in an alternate universe, it could have happened! in 1979, Michael Jackson's "Off the Wall" album was initially rejected by his label. It went on to sell over 20 million copies worldwide!

> **REMEMBER WHEN PEOPLE WERE PLANKING ON** anything and everything? in 2010, the internet craze of lying face-down with arms at one's side, known as "planking," had people posing in some of the most unusual places. It was an odd, yet wildly popular internet sensation!

> **CAN YOU WRAP YOUR HEAD AROUND THIS?** in 1995, a rumor spread that the iconic "Marilyn Monroe" dress worn by Madonna in her "Material Girl" music video was stolen. In reality, the dress was safely locked away in storage. Talk about fake news causing a commotion!

> **PICTURE THIS: IN THE 1980s, FRENCH** artist Thierry Noir began painting the Berlin Wall with bright, colorful faces. His work became a symbol of freedom and defiance, making Noir the first-ever street artist to paint the infamous wall. Who knew paint could be so powerful?

> **REMEMBER WHEN THE "MACARENA" DANCE** craze swept the world in the mid-90s? This catchy tune by Los del Río had everyone shaking their hips and flailing their arms in unison. Imagine the mayhem if tiktok was around then?

QUIRKS OF THE RICH & FAMOUS

> **CAN YOU IMAGINE A CELEBRITY PLAYING** with... dolls? Yep, you heard that right! in the early 2000s, actor Johnny Depp confessed to a peculiar hobby – collecting Barbie dolls! He even dressed them up as his famous characters like Jack Sparrow and Edward Scissorhands. Depp's collection has entertained his children and baffled many a guest at his home!

> **EVER HEARD OF SOMEONE KNITTING THEIR**
way to stardom? Well, actor Ryan Gosling sure has! This
heartthrob has an unusual affinity for knitting, a hobby
he picked up on the set of "Lars and the Real Girl" (2007).
It's said that he's often spotted knitting away in between
takes, leaving cast and crew both amused and impressed!

> **WHAT'S THAT BUZZING SOUND?**
Oh, it's just Scarlett Johansson and her hive of bees!
The actress took up beekeeping in 2018 as a way to help
save these crucial pollinators. Scarlett even gifted her
"Avengers" co-stars with jars of honey from her backyard
hive, turning them into fellow bee enthusiasts!

> **TALK ABOUT A SLIPPERY HOBBY!**
Nicolas Cage, the man of many quirks, once owned an
outrageous collection of exotic pets, including a pair of
king cobras named Moby and Sheba. Cage's neighbors must
have been on pins and needles, knowing that those slithery
serpents were just a stone's throw away!

> **MARILYN MONROE, THE QUINTESSENCE**
of silver screen glamour, had a secret struggle with the
camera. Despite her confident aura and iconic status, she
was known to be exceedingly camera-shy. Her co-star Don
Murray recalled how this Hollywood siren, loved by the
camera, would paradoxically suffer from a nervous rash
before filming. For someone who captivated audiences
with her apparent ease in front of the lens, it's a poignant
reminder that the glitter of celebrity often belies
the reality.

> **DID SOMEONE SAY... PIGEONS? YES, THAT'S**
right! Legendary boxer Mike Tyson has been an avid
pigeon fancier since childhood. He owns a coop of over

350 birds in New Jersey, and his feathered friends even helped him find solace during some of his darkest times. Neighbors, however, might not be as thrilled with the cooing cacophony!

> PICTURE THIS: TOM HANKS,

the beloved actor, typing away on an antique typewriter. Sounds like a scene from a movie, doesn't it? But it's true! Hanks has an impressive collection of over 250 vintage typewriters. We bet his pen pals are thrilled to receive typewritten letters with that old-school charm!

> MADONNA, THE QUEEN

of Pop, is also the queen of... cutlery? It's been reported that she insists on using a new toilet seat and her own set of utensils wherever she goes. Perhaps her entourage has grown accustomed to lugging around her personal porcelain throne and silverware!

> A SPOONFUL OF SUGAR MIGHT MAKE THE

medicine go down, but for Gwyneth Paltrow, a daily dose of bee stings keeps the doctor away! The actress and wellness guru swears by the ancient practice of apitherapy, which involves being stung by bees for therapeutic purposes. Talk about taking beauty treatments to a whole new level of buzzworthy!

> IMAGINE A BEAUTIFUL GARDEN FULL OF...

leeches? That's right! Demi Moore, the age-defying actress, has revealed that she uses leech therapy to detoxify her body and maintain her youthful glow. This blood-sucking treatment might make some people squirm, but for Demi, it's just another day at the spa!

> **PICTURE THIS: KESHA, THE POP SENSATION,** is known for her eccentricities, but she takes it to a whole new level with her hobby of crafting accessories from human teeth! Fans have sent her their extracted teeth, which she then turns into necklaces, earrings, and even clothing. Dental fashion never looked so... Interesting?

> **IF YOU THOUGHT OWNING SNAKES WAS** bizarre, wait until you hear about Nicolas Cage's other exotic pet – an octopus! The quirky actor spent a whopping $150,000 on this eight-legged wonder, believing it would help him with his acting skills. We can only imagine the strange bonding sessions between Cage and his tentacled friend!

> **DID SOMEONE SAY INVISIBLE ART?** That's correct! Actor and artist James Franco, known for pushing boundaries, once curated an entire art show featuring invisible sculptures and paintings. The exhibit, titled "Museum of Non-Visible Art," left visitors wondering if they were witnessing true art or a clever prank!

> **PICTURE THIS: THE KING OF POP,** Michael Jackson, once tried to buy the remains of Joseph Merrick, known as the "Elephant Man." He reportedly offered a staggering $1 million to acquire the skeletal remains from the Royal London Hospital. This macabre fascination surely adds to the long list of eccentricities attributed to the late pop icon.

> **ALLIGATORS AND HANDBAGS? THAT'S RIGHT!**
The legendary performer and sex symbol, Marilyn Monroe, once owned an alligator as a pet! It was a gift from none other than Arthur Miller, her playwright husband. Talk about an unconventional addition to the family!

> **CAN YOU IMAGINE SHARING YOUR** living space with a capybara, the world's largest rodent? Actress and model Ireland Baldwin, daughter of Alec Baldwin and Kim Basinger, has done just that! Her capybara, Clyde, even has his own instagram account, documenting his adventures with his famous owner.

> **THE LATE KING OF POP,** Michael Jackson, was known for his eccentricities, and his pet chimpanzee, Bubbles, was no exception. Bubbles lived a life of luxury at Neverland Ranch, wearing custom-made clothing and even eating at the dinner table with the family. He even accompanied Michael on tour, now that's what we call monkey business!

> **HOLD ONTO YOUR WHISKERS, BECAUSE THE** legendary surrealist artist Salvador Dalí had an ocelot named Babou as his trusty companion! Babou accompanied Dalí everywhere, including high-society events and even a voyage aboard the SS France. It's safe to say that Babou added a touch of the exotic to Dalí's already eccentric life!

INCREDIBLE FACTS FOR INQUISITIVE MINDS

> **ARE YOU READY FOR A HISS-TERICAL TALE?**
The late boxing legend Mike Tyson once owned a trio
of white Bengal tigers, named Kenya, Storm, and Boris.
The ferocious felines lived in luxurious custom-built
enclosures on Tyson's property, complete with waterfalls
and lush greenery. Talk about a knockout pet collection!

> **PICTURE THIS: "THE GODFATHER" STAR**
James Caan once owned a pet lion named Togar!
The magnificent beast lived with Caan in his Beverly
Hills home, where he would often take the lion for walks,
much to the astonishment of his neighbors. We can only
imagine the roar of excitement this unusual pet brought to
Caan's life!

CHAPTER SEVEN

FASCINATING CULTURAL FINDS!

DELECTABLE & NOT-SO-DELECTABLE DISHES

> **EVER BEEN CURIOUS ABOUT HOW TAR TASTES?** in Finland, they've got your back! Salty licorice, or "salmiakki," is a popular Finnish candy flavored with ammonium chloride, giving it a distinct, tar-like taste. This polarizing treat has inspired passionate debates among Finns, and you're either a die-hard fan or a staunch hater—there's no in-between!

> **FEAST ON THE FORMIDABLE FRIED TARANTULA,** a Cambodian delicacy hailing from Skuon. Initially a source of sustenance during the Khmer Rouge regime, these creepy crawlies have evolved into a sought-after snack. Tourists and locals alike crunch into the crispy legs and gooey abdomen with gusto. But are you brave enough to bite?

> **WHO NEEDS SLICED BREAD WHEN YOU'VE GOT** Iceland's geothermal rye bread? Known as "hverabrauð," this unique loaf is baked underground using the island's natural geothermal heat. Then, locals dig a hole, bury the dough, and let Mother Nature work her magic! The result? A sweet, dense bread that's a testament to Icelanders' ingenuity.

> **SARDINIA'S "CASU MARZU" IS NOT FOR THE** faint of heart or queasy stomachs. This sheep's milk cheese teems with live insect larvae, intentionally added

to promote fermentation. The larvae wriggle and writhe as the cheese breaks down, imparting a distinctive flavor. Diners must shield their eyes while eating, as the larvae can leap up to 6 inches when disturbed! Ready for a dining experience that's truly alive?

> EVER WISHED YOUR TOFU COULD WALK?

in Japan, you're in luck! "Ika shiokara," or fermented squid guts, is a dish that dances. When soy sauce comes in contact with the reaction, causing the squid tentacles to twitch and wriggle on the plate. Bon appétit, or should we say, "itadakimasu," to this quivering delight! Meet the infamous durian, a Southeast Asian fruit with a potent odor likened to rotten onions, gym socks, and even raw sewage. However, the taste is said to be heavenly – creamy, sweet, and custard-like. Are you willing to hold your nose and take a bite?

> SCOTLAND'S GOT A FISHY SECRET

up its sleeve: the fearsome haggis! This dish is made by stuffing a sheep's stomach with minced offal, oatmeal, suet, and spices before boiling it to perfection. Haggis has inspired Scottish poetry, Burns Night celebrations, and even tall tales of the elusive wild haggis, a fictional creature with legs of different lengths that roams the Highlands. Care for a taste of culinary lore?

> ARE YOU READY TO

swallow a beating heart? in Vietnam, "tiet canh," or raw blood soup, takes the concept of freshness to a whole new level. Typically made with duck or goose blood, the dish is often garnished with fresh herbs and served alongside the animal's still-beating heart. This chilling concoction is believed to boost virility and strength. Would you dare to slurp it down?

> **FORGET KFC, SOUTH KOREA'S** "sannakji" is where the actions at! This dish features live baby octopus, dismembered and served immediately, ensuring the tentacles are still wriggling as you eat. Be cautious, though – the suction cups can latch onto your throat, posing a choking hazard. A little danger with dinner, anyone?

> **ESCAMOLES, OR MEXICAN ANT LARVAE, ARE** often called "insect caviar." Harvested from the roots of agave plants, these edible insect eggs have been enjoyed by locals since the time of the Aztecs. With a buttery, nutty taste, escamoles are often sautéed with garlic and spices and served in tacos. Who's ready for a crunchy culinary adventure?

> **THE ITALIAN ISLAND OF SARDINIA IS BACK** at it again, this time with "su filindeu," an ultra-rare pasta so intricate that less than 10 people on Earth can make it by hand! Translating to "threads of God," this delicate pasta is crafted from a single strand of dough, stretched and folded repeatedly until it forms a fine, angel-hair-like lattice. Will you join the quest for this divine dish?

> **TAKE A TRIP TO JAPAN TO FEAST ON** "shirako," or fish sperm sacs. These creamy, custard-like sacs are served raw, fried, or steamed, often as a sushi

topping or in a warm sake broth. Rich in protein and vitamins, shirako is considered a delicacy in Japanese cuisine. Are you brave enough to sample this slippery surprise?

> **LOOKING FOR AN ODD DISH THAT REALLY** bites back? Try "yin-yang fish," a Taiwanese dish that's prepared by deep-frying a fish so quickly that its head remains alive while its body is cooked. The fish is served on a plate, mouth gaping and gills flapping as diners dig into the crispy flesh. An extreme example of freshness or just plain freaky? You decide.

> **HOLD ONTO YOUR APPETITES BECAUSE WE'RE** diving into the deep end with "drunken shrimp" from China! These feisty crustaceans are served live, often swimming in a bowl of strong liquor to momentarily stun them. Diners must act quickly to pop the tipsy shrimp into their mouths, as they can awaken and wriggle away. Ready for a mouthful of tipsy trouble?

> **EVER FANCIED EATING A CACTUS? IN MEXICO,** "nopales" are a staple ingredient in many dishes. These prickly pear cactus pads are carefully de-spined, sliced, and cooked, boasting a taste similar to green beans and a texture like okra. Nopales have long been praised for their numerous health benefits, but watch out for those pesky spines!

> **CALLING ALL DAREDEVILS! PERU'S "CUY,"** or guinea pig, might just be your next culinary conquest. Often served whole, roasted, or deep-fried, cuy has been a staple protein source in the Andes for thousands of years. In fact, some Peruvian homes even have guinea pig hutches for home-raised cuy. Will you take a nibble on this furry friend?

> **Ever wondered what it's like to eat**
a bee? in Japan, "hachinoko" or baby bee larvae, are
harvested from beehives and simmered in soy sauce and
sugar, resulting in a sweet, crunchy, and protein-packed
treat. Consumed for centuries, these buzzing bites are now
a rare and expensive delicacy. Care for a taste of the hive?

> **Let's get batty with Guam's "fruit bat**
soup"! Yes, you read that right – entire fruit bats are
boiled in a coconut milk broth, fur, wings, and all. The dish
is said to have a strong, gamey taste, and diners must
watch out for sharp bones and teeth. So, will you be brave
enough to slurp down a bowl of bat?

> **Why not chomp on some "century eggs"?**
in China, these preserved duck, chicken, or quail eggs
are left to ferment in a mixture of clay, ash, salt,
and quicklime for weeks or even months. The result is
a greenish-black, translucent jelly-like egg with a strong
sulfuric odor. Century eggs have graced Chinese tables
for centuries, but can you stomach this pungent bite
of history?

> **Fancy a taste of ancient Roman**
cuisine? "Garum," a fermented fish sauce, was the ketchup
of its time, used to flavor a wide variety of dishes. Made
by fermenting fish guts and salt in the sun for several
weeks, the pungent liquid was once a highly sought-after
commodity. Modern-day chefs have begun reviving this
long-lost condiment, so why not give it a whirl?

> **Behold the "black ivory coffee" from**
Thailand! Made from beans that have passed through the
digestive system of elephants, this unusual brew is said
to have a unique and nuanced flavor. The fermentation

process within the elephant's stomach imparts a distinct taste to the beans, making this coffee one of the most expensive and rare in the world. Fancy a cup of this seriously wild java?

LITTLE KNOWN TRAVEL & CULTURAL CUSTOMS

> BABY JUMPING, ANYONE?
"El Colacho" is a bizarre Spanish tradition where men dressed as the devil leap over rows of infants to cleanse them of evil spirits. Parents willingly place their newborns on mattresses for this daring ritual. Would you trust El Colacho with your little one?

> ON THE INDONESIAN
island of Bali, "Nyepi" is a day of complete silence, self-reflection, and fasting. The island shuts down for 24 hours; even the airport closes! Locals and tourists alike must stay indoors, with no lights, noise, or entertainment. Could you handle a day of utter quietude?

> TIME FOR A LITTLE HAIR-RAISING ACTION!
in india, the "Thaipusam" festival sees devotees piercing their bodies with hooks and skewers to show their devotion to the Hindu god Murugan. These intense piercings are believed to be painless due to divine intervention. Are you ready to bear witness to this astonishing display of faith?

> **IN TURKMENISTAN, THE "DOOR TO HELL"**
awaits! This fiery, gas-fueled crater has been burning
non-stop since 1971 when it was ignited by Soviet
geologists. The mesmerizing, glowing pit is a jaw-dropping
sight to behold. Will it ever stop burning?

> **BEHOLD THE SURREAL "CAT ISLAND"**
in Japan! Aoshima Island boasts
a population of over 100 cats
outnumbering humans six
to one. Originally brought
to the island to control
the rodent population,
these feline inhabitants
now reign supreme. Are
you ready to be ruled by
these fluffy overlords?

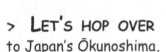

> **LET'S HOP OVER**
to Japan's Ōkunoshima,
fondly nicknamed "Rabbit Island."
Here, the bunnies are the bosses, outnumbering humans
at a rate that's off the official rabbit charts. These
cuddly commanders are the descendants of just few
released pets, and now they're hopping their way into
visitors hearts.

> **IN THE PHILIPPINES, THE ANNUAL**
"Crucifixion Festival" takes religious devotion to an
extreme level. Participants willingly endure crucifixion
by being nailed to crosses, replicating the suffering of
Jesus Christ. This shocking ritual has attracted curious
onlookers from around the world.

> **HAVE YOU EVER HEARD OF "BULLET ANT**
Gloves"? in the Brazilian Amazon, the indigenous
Satere-Mawe tribe practices a coming-of-age ritual that
involves wearing gloves filled with bullet ants, whose bites
are considered one of the most painful in the insect kingdom.
Young men must endure this agony to prove their strength
and resilience. Do you have what it takes to brave the bite?

> **IN THE REPUBLIC OF VANUATU,**
"Land Diving" is an adrenaline-pumping tradition. Men
leap from wooden towers with vines tied to their
ankles, plummeting headfirst toward the ground. This
death-defying custom is said to have inspired modern
bungee jumping. Are you ready to take the plunge for
tradition's sake?

> **IN THE HIGHLANDS OF PAPUA NEW GUINEA,**
the "Dani Tribe" practices a heart-wrenching custom
called "Finger Cutting." To express grief and pay tribute
to deceased loved ones, female tribe members amputate
a portion of their fingers.

LESSER KNOWN COUNTRIES

> **HAVE YOU EVER HEARD OF NAURU,**
the world's smallest island nation? Located in the Pacific
Ocean, Nauru has an area of only 8.1 square miles and
a population of around 10,000. Once rich in phosphate
deposits, the island's economy took a nosedive when the
resources were depleted, leaving behind a lunar-like
landscape. Can you imagine living on such a tiny
speck of land?

> THE TINY EUROPEAN NATION OF

Liechtenstein has a curious claim to fame: it's the world's largest producer of false teeth! This dental powerhouse manufactures an estimated 20% of the world's dentures. Who knew that such a small country could make such a significant impact on global smiles?

> ESWATINI, FORMERLY KNOWN AS SWAZILAND,

is one of the world's last absolute monarchies. The reigning king, Mswati III, has the power to dissolve parliament, and he traditionally chooses his wives from among the participants of the annual "Reed Dance" ceremony. Are you ready for a royal whirlwind of tradition and power?

> THE TINY AFRICAN

country of Djibouti is home to the world's second-lowest point, Lake Assal, which sits 509 feet below sea level. This saline wonder is saltier than the Dead Sea, with salt crystals forming surreal formations along its shores.

> THE SMALL SOUTH AMERICAN NATION OF

Suriname is a linguistic melting pot. With Dutch as its official language and over 20 recognized languages spoken throughout the country, Suriname is a fascinating blend of cultures. You might overhear snippets of Sranan Tongo, Javanese, or Chinese Hakka while visiting.

> ## TUVALU, A POLYNESIAN ISLAND NATION,

has a unique source of income: leasing its internet domain extension, ".tv," to television networks and streaming services. This digital goldmine has become a significant revenue stream for the tiny country. It's also one of the smallest countries in the world, at just 26 km^2.

> ## ANDORRA, A TINY NATION NESTLED

in the Pyrenees mountains between France and Spain, has a peculiar quirk: it boasts the world's highest life expectancy at 83.5 years. With clean mountain air and a relaxed pace of life, it seems that Andorra has discovered the secret to longevity. Would you want the Andorran way of life?

> ## KIRIBATI, AN ISLAND NATION IN THE

Pacific, straddles both the Equator and the international Date Line. This geographic oddity means that at certain times of the year, you can stand with one foot in today and the other in tomorrow It's a bucket list experience for the adventurous!

> ## BHUTAN, A SMALL KINGDOM NESTLED

in the Eastern Himalayas, measures its success not in GDP but in Gross National Happiness. This unique metric seeks to balance economic growth with the well-being of its citizens and the environment. Are you ready to embrace the pursuit of happiness in Bhutan?

> ## THE AFRICAN NATION OF LESOTHO IS

the only country in the world that lies entirely above 1,000 meters in elevation. This "Kingdom in the Sky" is known for its breathtaking mountain landscapes and unique cultural traditions. Can you envision the lofty majesty of Lesotho?

FASCINATING CULTURAL FINDS!

UNFORGETTABLE FESTIVALS & CELEBRATIONS

> **YOU'VE HEARD OF HORSE RACING, BUT HAVE** you ever witnessed camel racing? in the United Arab Emirates, the prestigious Al Marmoom Heritage Festival showcases these speedy, humpbacked animals as they race for glory. Grab your binoculars and hold onto your saddle!

> **THE SKIES OF ALBUQUERQUE, NEW MEXICO,** burst into color during the annual international Balloon Fiesta. This nine-day spectacle sees hundreds of hot air balloons from around the world take flight, creating a dazzling aerial display. How's that for an uplifting experience?

> **THAILAND'S SONGKRAN FESTIVAL TAKES** water fights to a whole new level! This annual event, which marks the Thai New Year, sees locals and visitors alike dousing each other with water. Anything goes, from water guns to buckets. This festival is to cleanse away bad luck. Would you take part in this nation wide water fight?

> **THE SMALL TOWN OF IVREA, ITALY,** has a smashing tradition: the Battle of the Oranges! This annual event sees teams of locals pelt each other with juicy oranges, recreating a historic uprising against tyranny. Are you prepared to taste sweet victory?

> **WELCOME TO THE WORLD'S COLDEST** festival: the Harbin international Ice and Snow Sculpture Festival in China! With towering ice sculptures, intricate snow carvings, and even an entire city made of ice, this frosty extravaganza is a winter wonderland like no other.

INCREDIBLE FACTS FOR INQUISITIVE MINDS

> **BUCKLE UP FOR THE QUIRKY**
"Kanamara Matsuri" in Kawasaki, Japan! This annual
fertility festival celebrates a unique centerpiece:
the phallus. From giant statues to candies and trinkets,
this phallic-themed event attracts visitors from around
the globe. Who knew a festival could be so, ahem,
uplifting?

> **IN DENMARK, BEING SINGLE ON YOUR 25TH**
birthday means being doused in cinnamon! Friends
and family ambush the birthday celebrant with copious
amounts of cinnamon as a light-hearted prank. Careful
not to sneeze your way through this spicy celebration!

> **LOVE A GOOD FOOD FIGHT? "LA TOMATINA"**
in Buñol, Spain, is a massive tomato-throwing event that
takes place each August. Thousands of participants pelt
each other with overripe tomatoes, turning the streets
into a sea of red pulp. Bring your goggles and prepare
for a saucy showdown!

THE LANGUAGE OF LOVE & OTHER RELATIONSHIP REVELATIONS

> **DID YOU KNOW THAT DURING THE VICTORIAN**
era, lovers exchanged "vinegar valentines"? These snarky,
satirical cards mocked and criticized the recipient,
often pointing out their flaws. Ouch, Cupid's arrow
sure stings!

> **BRACE YOURSELF FOR A LOVE OVERLOAD!**
South Korea isn't content with just one Valentine's Day—
they celebrate a whopping twelve "love days" throughout
the year! Each day has its own unique theme, from Hug Day
to Kiss Day and the ever-enchanting White Day. Think you
can keep up with this romantic whirlwind?

> **IN 15TH-CENTURY FRANCE, A PECULIAR**
device called a "love letter vending machine" was
all the rage! This ornate contraption, known as
a "Dial-a-Love-Letter," allowed suitors to create custom,
romantic messages by rotating dials. How's that for an
analog Tinder?

> **SURPRISING STATISTIC: ACCORDING TO**
a study, couples who meet online have a higher chance
of staying together than those who meet through
traditional means. Who knew that love could blossom
in cyberspace?

> **THE DANISH DATING CUSTOM OF "LOVESPOONS"**
is a heartwarming tradition. These intricately carved
wooden spoons were gifted by suitors to the object of
their affection as a symbol of commitment. Spooning has
never been so romantic!

> **IN 18TH-CENTURY**
England, a "bundling board"
was used to separate young
couples who shared a bed before
marriage. This wooden plank kept
the lovebirds physically apart,
ensuring their courtship
remained chaste. Talk about
a literal barrier to love!

> **THE HIMBA TRIBE OF NAMIBIA HAS**
a unique courtship ritual: the "Okujepisa Omukazendu,"
which translates to "offering a wife to a guest." Married
Himba women can choose to have consensual, short-term
relationships with visiting male guests, all with their
husband's approval. Now that's a different approach to
hospitality!

> **THE TIDONG PEOPLE OF INDONESIA HAVE**
a strange wedding custom: the bride and groom are
forbidden from using the bathroom for three days and
nights following their nuptials! This test of endurance is
believed to bring good luck and a strong marriage. Can you
hold on to love?

> **IN MAURITANIA, A LARGER BRIDE IS**
considered more desirable, leading to the practice of
"Leblouh," where young girls are fattened up for marriage.
This controversial custom is rooted in the belief that
a well-fed wife is a sign of wealth and prosperity. Can love
truly be measured in pounds?

> **THE BLACKENING IS A MESSY SCOTTISH**
pre-wedding tradition where the bride and groom are
covered in disgusting substances like rotten food and tar
by their friends. The couple is then paraded around town,
enduring public humiliation for good luck. Are you willing to
get dirty for love?

CHAPTER EIGHT

CURIOUS ANIMALS & NATURAL WONDERS

WEIRD & WONDERFUL
CRITTERS

> **DID YOU KNOW THAT THE MAJESTIC BLUE** whale's heart is as big as a small car? This quiet giant's heart pumps about 220 liters of blood with each beat—its aorta is so wide that a fully-grown human could swim right through it!

> **THE ELECTRIC EEL GENERATES A STUNNING** 860 volts of electricity! That is over five times a standard wall socket, which only delivers about 120 volts! These slippery fish use this shocking ability to zap predators or prey, and to navigate and communicate with each other.

> **THE TINY MICRO-ANIMAL CALLED THE** tardigrade, (also known as the "water bear,") can survive in extreme conditions! These microscopic marvels (about as big as a period at the end of this sentence) can endure boiling water, freezing temperatures, and even the vacuum of space.

> **HAVE YOU HEARD THAT AN OCTOPUS CAN** squeeze its entire body through a hole only the size of its beak? These flexible friends are completely boneless, (the beak is made of chitin) allowing them to compress into impossibly tight spaces. Talk about being the ocean's star contortionist!

> **GET READY TO BE ASTOUNDED BY THE FACT** that the jellyfish can revert back to its juvenile form after it has reached maturity. This remarkable creature

INCREDIBLE FACTS FOR INQUISITIVE MINDS

can cycle between both its adult and juvenile states indefinitely—essentially making it biologically immortal! Bet the scientists are studying that, most people would love to be immortal! Some current species of jellyfish are older than the dinosaurs. The mysterious comb jelly is thought to have first appeared on Earth around 500 million years ago.

> **Dolphins have unique "names" for each** other—they use distinct whistle patterns called echolocation to identify one another through a wide range of sounds and gestures. Who knew underwater chit-chat could be so personal and so sophisticated?

> **The amphibian quite like the** salamander, the axolotl, has the extraordinary ability to regenerate its limbs, heart, and even parts of its brain. These aquatic superstars are the ultimate masters of regeneration. If only we could grow a new finger after a paper cut!

> **Did you know that some** species of frog can freeze solid during winter and then thaw out in the spring, remaining completely unharmed? These chilly amphibians will survive temperatures below zero thanks to a natural "antifreeze" in their blood.

> **Can you believe that an Arctic whale,** the narwhal's iconic "tusk" is actually a giant tooth! These marine unicorns use their extraordinary dental protrusion to sense changes in their environment and even communicate with one another. Narwhales can grow as long as 17 feet and can weigh up to 4,200 pounds.

> **IT'S CRAZY TO THINK THAT IT'S THE MALE**
seahorse who gets pregnant and gives birth to it young.
These unique aquatic dads carry the eggs in their pouch
until the little seahorses are ready to be born. That is
definitely gender equality in the animal kingdom!

> **LET'S GLIMPSE THE WORLD OF THE**
blobfish—a deep sea creature that looks like it's having
a perpetual bad day! Sometimes called the "World's Ugliest
Animal", this gelatinous grump lives down in the ocean
abyss off the Australian coast, where it hangs out on the
sea floor, barely moving a muscle. The blobfish's jiggly,
low-density flesh allows it to survive the crushing pressure
down that deep, up to 9,200 feet—nearly three kilometres!

> **GET READY FOR THE FANG-TASTIC VIPERFISH,**
a creature that gives Dracula a run for his money! With
its massive, needle-like teeth and glowing photophores
(organs that produce light), this deep-sea predator lures
unsuspecting prey with light from the tip of its dorsal
ray—like a creepy underwater disco. The viperfish has
an elastic stomach and body skin so it can eat large prey,
which are usually other fish, so it is a cannibal too!

> **DID YOU KNOW THAT THE HUMBLE BUT**
important honeybee is known to recognize human
faces? These buzzy bodies use their
incredible memories to associate
specific faces with sources of
food. Next time you see a bee,
remember, it just might be
recognizing you!

> **THE INCREDIBLY STURDY DUNG BEETLE CAN** pull objects up to 1,141 times its own tiny body weight, (up to 3.5 ounces). To put that in perspective, it's like a human dragging along the ground six double-decker buses! These little powerhouses are nature's strongest insects.

> **THE MIGHTY YET TINY BOMBARDIER BEETLE,** when defending itself, can shoot a sizzling hot chemical spray from its rear end at its foe! This aggressive defense mechanism can reach temperatures of up to 212 degrees Fahrenheit, stunning it's foe mid attack! Now that's a hot topic!

> **YOU MIGHT BE AMAZED TO DISCOVER THAT** little ants have two stomachs. These industrious insects use one stomach for storing food to share with their colony, and the other for their own personal digestion. Ants are team players to the extreme, try not eating just for two, but for hundreds!

> **DID YOU KNOW THAT SINGLE TERMITE QUEEN** can lay an egg every 15 second! That means she produces over 6,000 eggs each day! These regal insects are definitely the egg-laying champions of the insect world.

> **HAVE YOU HEARD OF THE GIRAFFE WEEVIL?** Hailing from Madagascar, this peculiar bug sports an absurdly long neck—like a miniature, six-legged giraffe! But don't underestimate its quirky appearance; the giraffe weevil uses its elongated neck to win over the ladies and build elaborate leaf nests. Who knew that having a giraffe-like neck could be such a hit in the insect dating scene?

> **THE ELEGANT YET DEADLY ORCHID MANTIS**
is here to tickle your funny bone! This fabulous insect looks like it stepped right off the fashion show runway, disguised as a stunning orchid flower. The orchid mantis uses its vibrant colors and petal-shaped limbs to lure in prey, ambush at every meal. Talk about a killer sense of style!

> **TERMITES ARE REAL ROCK 'N' ROLL INSECTS.**
They communicate by banging their heads against their nest walls, creating vibrational signals. That's right, these little critters are the original headbangers, jamming to their own beat and keeping their fellow termites in the loop. Who knew the insect world could be so metal?

> **THE SNEAKY ANTICS OF THE MYRMARACHNE,**
or ant-mimicking jumping spider is sure to amuse you! This eight-legged trickster has mastered the art of deception, disguising itself as an ant to fool both predators and prey. With its clever costume and ant-like movements, this spider even hangs out with ants without raising suspicion. Talk about an undercover agent with a taste for flies, moths and crickets—tiny, six-legged hors d'oeuvres!

> **READY FOR A HEARTWARMING FACT?**
Penguins mate for life and sing unique "songs" to find their partners in the feathery crowd. Each penguin's distinct call helps them reunite in a sea of black and white. Now that's true love!

> **THE COLLECTIVE NOUN FOR A GROUP OF**
flamingos is called a "flamboyance"? These pink party animals definitely know how to make a statement with their vibrant colors and unique, one-legged poses. If that's not flamboyant, then what is?

INCREDIBLE FACTS FOR INQUISITIVE MINDS

> **DID YOU KNOW THAT THE BLACK BIRD,**
the crow, can recognize itself in a mirror? These brainy
birds are part of an elite club of self-aware animals, which
also includes humans, apes, and dolphins. Mirror, mirror on
the wall, who's the smartest bird of them all?

> **OWLS HAVE TUBULAR-SHAPED EYES THAT GIVE**
them extraordinary night vision. These nocturnal bird
hunters have eyeballs so large, that they can't move
in their sockets. Owls are known for their fixed stare!

> **WHAT BIRD MIGRATES FURTHER THAN ANY OTHER**
bird on Earth? Answer; The Arctic Tern. These incredible
avian adventurers travel 25,000 miles from their Arctic
breeding grounds to their winter home in Antarctica each
year. Now they are definitely
called frequent flyers!

> **THE MIGHTY BALD EAGLE**
has a wingspan of up to eight feet!
These majestic birds can soar at
altitudes of up to 10,000 feet and reach flying
speeds of up to 100 miles per hour. Eagle-eyed,
they are top avian predators—hold onto your hats
if you look up and see one circling!

> **BUCKLE UP, BIRD-LOVERS, MAKE**
way for the speedster of the skies: the
peregrine falcon! This feathered daredevil
can reach speeds of over 240 mph (386 km/h) when
diving to catch its prey, making it the fastest animal
on Planet Earth.

> **INTRODUCING THE LYREBIRD, THE MASTER**
impersonator in the bird world! This talented Aussie
species can mimic a vast array of sounds, from other birds'

calls to chainsaws, car alarms, and even camera shutters. If you are in the Australian bush hearing a bizarre symphony of noises, it might just be the amazing local lyrebird trying to impress you with its vocal prowess!

> **HERE'S A LESSER-KNOWN BIRD FACT THAT'LL** ruffle your feathers: Did you know that birds can see a wider range of colors than us humans? Thanks to their additional color receptor cone, our feathery friends can perceive ultraviolet light, allowing them to see a kaleidoscope of colors that remain invisible to us. So, when you spot a bird gazing at the sky or a blossoming tree, just remember they're enjoying a vibrant visual spectacle beyond our earthbound capability!

> **THE WORLD'S SMALLEST MAMMAL IS THE** near-threatened bumblebee bat of which we have about 5,100 individuals left in the wild. This pint-sized wonder weighs a mere two grams and has a wingspan of just six inches. Classed as harmless this bat can be called "cute".

> **CAN YOU BELIEVE THAT THE COLOR-CHANGING** chameleon can move each eye independently of the other? This extraordinary and unique ability gives them a 360-degree view of their environment—what an eye-opening experience!

> **THE UNSUSPECTING SNAIL** can fall sleep for up to three years? These sluggish molluscs enter a state of hibernation to conserve energy when food is scarce, power napping in the house that travels on their back!

INCREDIBLE FACTS FOR INQUISITIVE MINDS

> **YOU MIGHT BE SURPRISED TO KNOW THAT**
a plant in the mint family called catnip, which makes cats
go wild, actually has a calming effect on humans. This
fascinating plant contains a compound called nepetalactone,
which can reduce anxiety and help humans relax. We should
probably leave it to the cats though!

> **HAVE YOU HEARD ABOUT THE VERY CLEVER**
animal duo—the honeyguide bird and the honey badger?
This feathery scout leads the way to bee hives that it can
see from on high so its fearless partner can use its sharp
badger claws to break open the hive. The bird then feasts
on the beeswax and larvae, while the honey badger indulges
in the sweet, golden honey! What an example of teamwork
making the dream work!

> **WHAT ABOUT THE WEIRD AND WONDERFUL**
world of the pistol shrimp and the goby fish? These
unlikely BFFs share a watery dwelling where the shrimp
keeps house while the goby stands guard. In exchange
for its construction skills, the shrimp relies on the goby's
keen eyesight to warn it of any approaching predators.
Together, they form a perfect partnership—opposites
really do attract!

> **AND ANOTHER MARVELOUS ALLIANCE EXISTS**
between the clownfish and the sea anemone! This dynamic
duo has forged a unique bond—the clownfish finds shelter
among the stinging tentacles of the anemone, (which
are lethal to other fish, but the clownfish is immune).
In return, the clownfish defends its host from predators
and provides it with tasty leftovers. So, it's definitely
a case of love thy anemone! Shout out to Nemo!

> **You'll probably giggle at the oxpecker**
bird and its large herbivore buddies! This avian
chiropractor perches on the backs of animals like buffalo
and giraffes to feast on the pesky ticks and other insect
parasites that plague them. The oxpecker gets a free menu
and the herbivores enjoy a much-needed cleansing spa day.
It's a win-win situation for all critters involved!

> **A similar arrangement can be found**
between the cleaner wrasse and its clients in the
underwater world! These helpful little fish set up "cleaning
stations" where they remove parasites, dead skin, and
debris from other fish swimming by. Their clients tread
water, patiently waiting their turn for a deep clean.
The wrasse is well fed, and its fishy clients leave with
a fresh, healthy glow—now that's a symbiotic relationship
to make a splash about!

> **Get ready for a jaw-dropping discovery:**
the hairy frog, aka the "horror frog," when threatened by
a predator, takes self-defense to a whole new level! This
amphibious action hero actually breaks its own toe bones,
which then pierce through the skin to form makeshift
claws to fight off the attack! Talk about going Wolverine
to survive in the wild!

> **Behold the cunning hognose snake, the**
ultimate drama queen of the reptile world! When
confronted up close by predators, this crafty serpent
puts on an Oscar-winning performance, writhing in fake
agony and even releasing a foul-smelling musk odor which
mimics the scent of death. The predator is fooled by this
masterful ruse and leaves the "deceased" snake alone,
allowing it to live and die again another day!

INCREDIBLE FACTS FOR INQUISITIVE MINDS

> **THE BIZARRE SURVIVAL TECHNIQUE OF THE**
hibernating Arctic ground squirrel just has to be
mentioned here! This chilly critter can successfully
regulate its body temperature down to below freezing—
about 27°F (-3°C)—and avoid turning into a furry ice-block
during the harsh Arctic winter. This ice-cold strategy
means it'll emerge unscathed, ready to play and mate in the
springtime tundra!

> **THE MIMIC OCTOPUS IS**
a master or mistress of disguise—it
can change not only its color but
also its very shape to impersonate
other sea-dwelling animals! When
threatened, this underwater
escape artist can transform
itself into a flounder, a venomous
lionfish, even a sea snake—just
by contorting its flexible body.
That's a shape-shifting survival
skill worthy of a round of applause!

> **YOU WILL BE ASTONISHED BY THE**
self-sacrificing strategy of the Malaysian exploding ant!
When their colony is under threat, these devoted insects grab
hold of their enemies and rupture their very own abdomens,
releasing a sticky, toxic goo in self-defense. This is the
ultimate act of kamikaze bravery—the ants give their tiny
lives to protect their tiny comrades. That is very big of them!

> **MEET THE AWE-INSPIRING POWER OF THE**
Jesus Christ lizard, a reptile found in the rainforests
of Central America which has a miraculous talent! This
little-known critter, also known as the common basilisk,
can sprint across the surface of the water on its hind

legs—like it's walking on water! This nimble lizard has developed specialized feet that create pockets of air, keeping it afloat as it dashes away from danger. So, let's raise a toast to this astonishing reptile that's truly walking on water!

> **CATS DON'T JUST PURR WHEN THEY'RE pleased - there's a** real science behind this soothing sound. Purring is created by the vibration of the vocal folds when the feline breathes in and out. Fascinatingly, purring frequencies have been found to promote healing and reduce pain in the cat's body. So, when your kitty settles down for a purr session on your lap, they're not just happy - they're also doing a mini workout!

> **WHO KNEW ANTS COULD BREAK SPEED records? Meet** the Saharan silver ant, the world's fastest ant, found in the scorching desert of Tunisia. These little speed demons can travel a meter per second - that's like you sprinting over 200 miles per hour! They've evolved this super speed to survive the scorching desert temperatures - talk about being hot on your feet!

> **STEP ASIDE, BLUE WHALES, BECAUSE THE** Argentinosaurus, hailing from the late Cretaceous period about 94 to 97 million years ago, might just have you beat in the size department. This gigantic vegetarian dinosaur stretched up to 120 feet long from nose to tail, making it longer than three school buses parked end to end. It's so big, its heart was the size of a refrigerator—now, that's a lot of dinosaur love from millions of years past!

> **BEHOLD, THE FOUR-WINGED-WONDER!** About 120 million years ago, this feathered phenom flitted through the forests of what is now China. The Microraptor

boasted not just two, but four wings—one set on its arms and another on its legs. This pint-sized pterosaur could glide gracefully between trees, perhaps snacking on unsuspecting insects or smaller critters below.

> **AROUND 68 TO 66 MILLION YEARS AGO,** a walking fortress roamed the earth. Its name? the Ankylosaurus. This guy had armor so tough, its body was covered with massive knobs and plates of bone, complete with a bashing club on its tail. Predators likely thought twice before messing with this prehistoric tank—talk about a heavy-duty herbivore!

> **PICTURE A TURKEY ON STEROIDS, AND YOU** might come close to the Therizinosaurus. This bizarre beast roamed the earth around 70 million years, around what is now Mongolia, the Therizinosaurus sported claws up to three feet long—longer than your average household sofa! It's thought these ginormous claws weren't just for catching dinner but for leaf stripping ...or perhaps making a prehistoric fashion statement?

MARVELOUS MAMMALS

> **WHAT IS FASTER THAN MOST SPORTS CARS?** The incredibly speedy cheetah is! This big cat can accelerate from 0 to 60 miles per hour in a mere 3 seconds! However, these sprinting kitties can only maintain their lightning-fast speed for short distances, so blink and you'll miss it!

> **GET READY FOR AN AUSTRALIAN FACT—**
kangaroos are simply unable to walk backward! These
hoppy hairy Aussies have a unique body structure with
large hind legs and a long, muscular tail which makes
reverse movement impossible. Kangaroos are consistently
forward thinking!

> **DID YOU KNOW THAT THE COLOSSAL FEMALE**
African elephant has a pregnancy that lasts nearly two
years—22 months? That's the longest gestation period
of any other land mammal. The titanic babies are born
weighing a hefty 200 pounds and already standing three
feet tall!

> **WHOSE TONGUE CAN STRETCH OVER TWO FEET**
in length? The ludicrously long tongue of the giant
anteater can! It is perfect for slurping up ants and
termites from their deep underground homes. Talk about
a tongue-twister!

> **THE PLUCKY PLATYPUS IS ONE OF THE FEW**
mammals on Planet Earth that lay eggs. These quirky
creatures are an egg-ception to the mammalian rule,
as most mammals give birth to live young. Along with
their equally odd echidna friends, they are known as
monotremes. The platypus also has a poisonous spike in its
leg, ready to deploy at a moment's notice, so watch out if
you see one!

> **DID YOU KNOW THAT SLOTHS ONLY POOP**
once a week? These slow-moving creatures take their
sweet time digesting food in the trees, and when they
finally need to go, they make a perilous journey to the
ground, risking their lives to predators—now that's
commitment to a bathroom break!

> **YOU MIGHT NOT KNOW THAT BATS ARE THE** only mammals capable of sustained flight. While other mammals like flying squirrels, lemurs, and gliding possums are capable of gliding through the air, bats are the only ones capable of sustained and controlled flight. Some bats can fly at speeds of up to 99 miles per hour and can even fly up to 10,000 feet high!

> **GIRAFFES AND HUMANS HAVE THE SAME** number of neck vertebrae! Both species possess seven cervical vertebrae, but a giraffe's are obviously much larger, allowing for their iconic long necks. Darwin's theory of natural selection proposes that giraffes with long necks had an advantage for getting food from trees over species with shorter necks.

> **IF YOU THINK YOU EAT** quickly, prepare to be enthralled by the fact that the semi-aquatic star-nosed mole can eat worms and small insects much faster than the human eye can even follow! These peculiar creatures can identify and consume their prey in just 225 milliseconds! Who knew dining could be so speedy—that's one fast breakfast!

> **EVER SEEN A MAMMAL THAT LOOKS LIKE IT** was designed by committee? Meet the aardvark, a curious critter from Africa that sports a pig-like snout, rabbit-like ears, and a kangaroo-like tail. While they may appear to be hodgepodge of various creatures, aardvarks are perfectly adapted to their nocturnal, insect-eating lifestyle. Talk about making the best of what you've got!

> **MARVEL AT THE TINY BUT MIGHTY ETRUSCAN** shrew, weighing in at a mere 1.8 grams, making it the world's smallest mammal by mass. These petite powerhouses can be found scurrying about in the grasslands of Southern Europe and North Africa, scarfing down twice their body weight in insects every day. Size isn't everything, folks!

> **PICTURE A MARINE MAMMAL WITH** a grin that could win a beauty pageant. You've just imagined the charmingly toothy sea otter! Not only do these whiskered water lovers have the densest fur of any mammal, but they also use tools to crack open tasty shellfish—a skill once thought exclusive to primates. A round of applause for our furry marine multitaskers!

> **EVER HEARD OF A DEER THAT BARKS LIKE** a dog? Look no further than the muntjac deer of Southeast Asia! These small, solitary creatures have developed a unique barking call to alert each other of danger. With a bark like that, who needs antlers?

> **DID YOU KNOW THAT THE AFRICAN NAKED** mole-rat can live without oxygen for up to 18 minutes? These peculiar, hairless rodents have adapted to their low-oxygen subterranean environment by switching to a metabolic process typically found in plants. One might say they're the real sustainability warriors!

> **PICTURE A MAMMAL WITH ARMOR PLATING** that would put a knight to shame. Meet he peculiar pangolin, an insect-eating mammal covered in large, overlapping scales. These scaly creatures roll up into a ball when threatened, effectively turning into a living suit of armor. Knights in shining armor, eat your heart out!

> **DID YOU KNOW THAT THE LONG-NOSED**
proboscis monkey can swim underwater for several minutes
at a time? These aquatic primates can be found in the
mangrove forests of Borneo, using their impressive swimming
skills to escape predators. Surf's up, monkey dudes!

> **WHAT MAMMAL CAN HOLD ITS BREATH FOR**
nearly two hours while diving to depths of over
9,800 feet? The incredible Cuvier's beaked whale! These
deep-diving cetaceans can stay submerged longer and dive
deeper than any other mammal. No diving buddies required
for these aquatic adventurers!

> **IMAGINE A MAMMAL WITH TEETH SO SHARP**
they can slice through bone like butter. You've just
envisioned the ferocious Tasmanian devil, native to the
Australian island of Tasmania. These carnivorous marsupials
have powerful jaws and a bite force stronger than any other
mammal of their size. Bon appétit, little devils!

> **FANCY A MAMMAL WITH A BUILT-IN SNORKEL?**
Meet the Saiga antelope, whose large, flexible nose
acts as a natural air filter in dusty environments. These
odd-looking creatures roam the steppes of Central Asia,
turning heads with their unique facial features. With
a schnoz like that, who needs diving gear?

> **ARE YOU READY FOR A MAMMAL THAT CAN**
live over 200 years? The bowhead whale, native to the
Arctic, boasts the longest known lifespan of any mammal!
These massive creatures are also nicknamed "icebreakers"
for their ability to break through ice up to two feet thick.
Now that's what we call a cool character!

> **WHAT MAMMAL CAN ROTATE ITS HEAD NEARLY**
360 degrees? The enigmatic ring-tailed lemur from
Madagascar! These quirky primates use their impressive

flexibility to scan the environment for threats and communicate with others. Talk about having eyes in the back of your head!

> **CAN YOU GUESS WHICH MAMMAL HAS** a built-in winter coat? The Arctic fox has a thick, insulating fur that changes color with the seasons—white in winter and brownish-gray in summer. These cunning critters are the ultimate fashionistas of the tundra!

> **WHAT MAMMAL IS KNOWN FOR ITS** charismatic, complex songs? The humpback whale! These gentle giants sing intricate melodies that can last for hours and travel vast distances underwater. They're like the opera singers of the ocean, belting out tunes for all to hear!

> **CAN YOU GUESS WHICH MAMMAL CAN DRINK** up to 50 gallons of water in just three minutes? It's the dromedary camel from the deserts of North Africa and the Middle East! These humpbacked, desert-dwelling animals have a built-in hydration system perfect for surviving in arid environments. Cheers to that!

WACKY WILDERNESS & CLIMATE QUIRKS

> **INTRODUCING THE MYSTICAL "FAIRY CIRCLES"** of Namibia! These peculiar round patches of barren land surrounded by lush vegetation have puzzled scientists and inspired local folklore. The most recent scientific explanation? It's a turf war between termites and plants!

The subterranean insects munch away at the roots of plants, creating the circles, while the plants surrounding the circles grow more vigorously due to the increased water and nutrients. Who knew termites could be such landscape artists?

> **READY FOR A "HAIR-RAISING" EXPERIENCE?**
in Mexico's Cueva de los Cristales (Cave of the Crystals), discovered in April 2000, you'll find colossal gypsum crystals up to 39 feet (12 meters) long, weighing up to 55 tons! These gigantic crystal formations grow in the scorching heat (up to 150° F) and extreme humidity of the cave, resembling a scene straight out of a science fiction movie!

> **HAVE YOU HEARD OF THE PECULIAR**
"Sailing Stones" of Death Valley, California? These are enigmatic rocks that seem to move across the desert floor, leaving mysterious trails behind them. It turns out that this movement of the stones is caused by a combination of wind, thin ice sheets, and a slick, wet clay surface. The result is a slow-motion glide across the desert, leaving the stones' tracks for all to see!

> **BEHOLD THE PSYCHEDELIC BEAUTY OF THE**
geological wonder "Rainbow Mountains" in China's Zhangye Danxia Landform Geological Park! These multicolored mountains appear to be painted in a vivid array of tones, but their mesmerizing appearance is actually the result of millions of years of sandstone and mineral deposits pressed together which are then eroded by wind and rain. Mother Nature is the ultimate painter!

> **HOLD YOUR (SEA)HORSES! DID YOU KNOW**
that the ocean is home to the world's tallest mountain? It is mostly underwater... Mauna Kea in Hawaii is only

13,796 feet (4,205 meters) above sea level, but its true base lies 19,685 feet (6,000 meters) below the ocean's surface, making it even taller than Mount Everest!

> HERE'S A MIND-BENDING FACT: THE PRESSURE at the ocean's deepest point, the Challenger Deep in the Mariana Trench, beneath the western Pacific Ocean, is a whopping 1,086 atmospheres! With one atmosphere for every 10 meters of water depth, and one atmosphere being the pressure of 14.6 pounds at sea level, that's like stacking 50 jumbo jets on top of your head—talk about having a crush!

> IN THE 21ST CENTURY OVER 95% OF THE ocean remains unexplored will surely surprise you! With so much left to discover, who knows what mind-blowing secrets and scary sea creatures lie beneath the waves? Calling Captain Nemo—it's time for an adventure!

> HERE'S A HUMDINGER: THE OCEAN IS SO vast that it contains enough gold to give every person on Earth (about 8 billion of us) 9 pounds (4 kilograms) of the precious metal! But don't grab your snorkel just yet—extracting it would simply be an impossible task.

> READY TO BE AWESTRUCK BY THE MAGICAL Northern Lights? These celestial light shows were believed to be the spirits of ancestors dancing across the sky, according to many indigenous cultures across the Arctic. But it turns out that they are actually the result of solar particles colliding with atmospheric gases. These breathtaking displays are most common near the poles due to the Earth's magnetic field.

INCREDIBLE FACTS FOR INQUISITIVE MINDS

> **SALAR DE UYUNI IN BOLIVIA IS AN**
awe-inspiring salt flat that turns into a massive mirror
during the rainy season, reflecting the sky above with
astonishing precision. Spanning over 4,050 square miles
(10,500 square kilometers), this mesmerizing landscape
is considered to be a sacred place by the Aymara people,
native to the Andean region.

> **LUCKY YOU WEREN'T BLOWN AWAY BY THE**
Great Hurricane of 1780, the deadliest Atlantic
hurricane on record. This monstrous storm tore across
the Caribbean, killing an estimated 22,000 people,
leaving an awful trail of devastation in its wake.
With winds exceeding 200 mph (320 km/h), this
catastrophic storm remains a chilling reminder of
nature's unstoppable force.

> **WHAT ABOUT THE**
infamous Tri-State Tornado
of 1925? It was the
deadliest and longest-lasting
tornado (different to
a hurricane) in U.S. history!
This monstrous twister
rampaged through
Missouri, Illinois, and
indiana for an astonishing
219 miles (352 km),
flattening entire towns
and claiming nearly
700 lives. Its path of
destruction was so wide that some eyewitnesses mistook
it for a rolling cloud of black smoke! The tornado was

a mile wide at times, and the winds reached 300 miles per hour, (482 km/h) putting it at the top of the Fujita scale for tornado intensity!

> **YOU WILL SHIVER AT THE BONE-CHILLING** tale of the 1816 "Year Without a Summer"! Following the massive volcanic eruption of indonesia's Mount Tambora in 1815, the whole world experienced a sudden fall in temperatures, causing widespread crop failures and subsequent food shortages. This bizarre weather anomaly led to frost forming in July, snow in August, and even inspired Mary Shelley to write her iconic novel, "Frankenstein"!

> **HOLY HAILSTONES, BATMAN! DID YOU KNOW** the largest hailstone ever recorded in the United States fell in Vivian, South Dakota, on July 23, 2010? This icy ball weighed 1.94 pounds (0.88 kg) and measured a staggering 8 inches (20.3 cms) in diameter. Steel reenforced umbrellas anyone?

> **HAVE YOU HEARD OF BLOOD RAIN? IT IS AN** extremely rare weather event. In ancient Rome, people believed that blood rain was a terrifying spiritual omen. This eerie phenomenon turns the sky crimson, giving everything a spooky reddish hue. We know now that it's actually caused by desert dust or algae particles suspended in rainwater.

> **WELCOME TO THE WORLD OF BALL LIGHTNING!** This rare and unexplained phenomenon involves a glowing, spherical object varying from pea-sized to several meters in diameter, and is typically associated with thunderstorms. Ball lightning lasts longer than a bolt of lightning and can float in the air, pass through solid

INCREDIBLE FACTS FOR INQUISITIVE MINDS

objects, and even bounce around like a beach ball at a wild summer party! Scientists are still baffled by this shocking display of nature's power, making it one of the most mysterious weather events on Earth.

> **BRACE YOURSELVES FOR THE WORLD'S SNOWIEST** place, Aomori City in Japan, which gets pummeled with a mind-boggling average of 312 inches (7.92 meters) of snow each year! Talk about a never-ending snowball fight!

> **BRACE YOURSELVES FOR A SONIC BOOM!** The loudest sound ever recorded in history was the eruption of the Krakatoa volcano in indonesia in 1883. The explosion was so loud, it circled the Earth four times and was heard 3,000 miles away - that's like a sound made in New York being heard in Los Angeles!

> **EVER SEEN IT RAIN FISH? POWERFUL waterspouts or** tornadoes can, on rare occasions, lift aquatic animals like fish or frogs from waterways and then drop them miles away from their original locations. These "animal rains" have fallen all around the world, leaving slippery surprises on the doorsteps of locals. Just imagine looking out your window to find a school of fish flopping around on your lawn!

> **EVER DREAMED OF SEEING A BEACH GLOW in the dark?** Some islands in the Maldives offer this eerie yet enchanting spectacle! The glow is due to a type of plankton called bioluminescent phytoplankton. When disturbed, these tiny organisms emit a radiant blue light, turning the waves into a magical, twinkling light show. So, the next time you're in the Maldives, take a night swim and watch the ocean light up like a Christmas tree!

CHAPTER NINE

A WALK THROUGH HISTORY

WORLDS MARVELOUS
MONUMENTS

> CAN YOU BELIEVE THAT THE ICONIC EIFFEL
Tower in Paris was almost torn down? Originally intended
as just a temporary exhibit for the 1889 World's Fair, it
faced opposition from many locals who considered it an
eyesore. Today, the Eiffel Tower stands tall as a probably
one of the most beloved symbols of France. Imagine, Paris
without its iron lady?

> THE MYTH HAS BEEN BUSTED, AND WHILE
The Great Wall of China may not be visible from space it's
absolutely bizarre connection to sticky rice is certainly out
of this world! The mortar used to build parts of the wall
contains sticky rice, which strengthens its durability. Who
knew that one of the world's most famous landmarks had
a secret ninja ingredient?

> GUESS WHAT? THE LEANING TOWER OF
Pisa isn't the only tilting wonder in the world. The "Big Ben"
clock tower in London is leaning as well, albeit at a much
subtler angle of 0.26 degrees. It's said that the tilt is due
to decades of underground excavation in the area, causing
the tower's foundation to shift.

> THE STATUE OF LIBERTY, AN ENDURING
symbol of freedom, was a gift from France to the United
States. But did you know that her iconic green hue is the
result of natural weathering? The statue's copper exterior
has for reacted with the elements, forming a protective
patina over time. Who says oxidation can't be fashionable?

INCREDIBLE FACTS FOR INQUISITIVE MINDS

> **MOUNT RUSHMORE, THE COLOSSAL SCULPTURE** of four US presidents, is an impressive sight, but it's missing something – the presidents' bodies! The original design called for full-body sculptures, but due to funding constraints, only the heads were completed. Can you picture these stony-faced leaders with chiseled torsos?

> **ROME'S FAMOUS COLOSSEUM, ONCE THE SITE** of epic gladiator battles, had an innovative feature: a retractable roof! The ancient Romans used a complex system of ropes and pulleys to provide shade and shelter for spectators. Who knew that modern stadiums had a touch of ancient inspiration?

> **THE GREAT PYRAMID OF GIZA, THE OLDEST** and largest of the Egyptian pyramids, was once covered in smooth, polished limestone. This brilliantly bright casing made the pyramid shimmer in the sun, creating a dazzling sight. Can you imagine the blinding splendor of this ancient wonder?

> **GRAB YOUR GONDOLAS! VENICE, ITALY,** the city of canals, was founded way back in 421 AD and is built on over 100 small islands. Its foundations are supported by large wooden piles driven deep into the marshy ground. Despite the city's seemingly precarious position, it has endured for centuries, defying the odds and enchanting visitors for centuries now. A place where mystery, history, and romance intertwine, it no wonder why!

> CRAZY FACT: MACHU PICCHU, THE ANCIENT incan city perched high in the Andes Mountains of Peru, was never discovered by the Spanish conquistadors – as most assume. This "Lost City of the incas" remained hidden until 1911, when American explorer Hiram Bingham stumbled upon it while hiking. Can you fathom the thrill of uncovering a long-lost civilization?

> THE TOWER OF LONDON, a historic castle and former royal residence, is now home to the British Crown Jewels. But its bizarre secret is its resident ravens – legend has it that if the ravens ever leave the Tower, the British monarchy will fall. To keep the kingdom secure, the Tower employs a "Ravenmaster" to care for the birds. Are you ready for a feathered tale of royal intrigue?

> THE BEAUTIFUL TAJ MAHAL IN INDIA IS AN eternal symbol of love, built by Emperor Shah Jahan in memory of his wife Mumtaz Mahal. However, did you know that Shah Jahan planned to build an identical black marble mausoleum for himself across the river from the Taj Mahal? His plans were halted by his own son, who overthrew him and imprisoned him for life.

> THE SISTINE CHAPEL IN VATICAN CITY IS renowned for its stunning frescoes by Michelangelo. But a bizarre fact is that Michelangelo, a sculptor by trade, initially rejected the commission, believing he was being set up to fail by his rivals. Despite his reluctance,

he created one of the world's most breathtaking masterpieces. Can you imagine the drama behind this divine artwork?

WEIRD CLOTHING TRENDS OF THE PAST

> **ZOOT SUITS, THE FLASHY, OVERSIZED** outfits of the 1940s, were so controversial that they sparked a series of riots in Los Angeles! With their wide-legged pants and extravagant jackets, zoot suits became a symbol of rebellion for some and a fashion faux pas for others.

> **DID YOU KNOW THAT THE HUMBLE T-SHIRT** was once considered scandalous? in the early 20th century, it was merely an undergarment. It wasn't until the 1950s, when stars like James Dean and Marlon Brando rocked them on the big screen, that T-shirts became a sizzling-hot fashion statement.

> **HOLD ONTO YOUR PETTICOATS, LADIES!** The hoop skirt, a popular fashion trend in the 1800s, was known for causing quite a stir. These voluminous garments made it nearly impossible to pass through doors, and, in some cases, even caused accidents by knocking over furniture or small children!

> **DID YOU KNOW THAT IN THE 16TH AND** 17th centuries, women would wear a "bum roll" or "farthingale" to accentuate their hips? These padded

undergarments created an exaggerated hourglass silhouette that was all the rage among fashionable ladies of the time.

> **IF YOU THINK PLATFORM SHOES ARE**
a modern invention, think again! Chopines, a type of platform shoe with incredibly high soles, were popular among European women in the 15th to 17th centuries. Walking in these elevated shoes required assistance from servants, making them symbols of wealth and prestige. The higher the chopine, the higher the social status of the wearer. Talk about stepping up in the world!

> **EVER HEARD OF THE "HOBBLE SKIRT"?**
This bizarre fashion trend from the early 1900s featured a skirt that was so tight around the ankles, it forced women to take tiny, mincing steps. While the style was short-lived, it certainly left its mark as one of history's weirdest fashion trends!

> **HERE'S A HAIR-RAISING FACT FOR YOU:**
in the 18th century, powdered wigs, known as "perukes," were all the rage among European aristocrats. But what's even more bizarre is that these wigs were often infested with lice and other critters! To combat the itchiness, wig-wearers would carry around a tiny wooden rod called a "scratcher" to poke under their perukes and relieve the itch without messing up their fabulous hairdos. Talk about a hair-raising fashion statement!

> **SO THIS TREND IS IN AGAIN? ANCIENT**
Romans, fashion-forward as they were, were the first to wear socks with sandals! They rocked the look with their woolen socks and open-toed sandals, turning heads in the 2nd century AD.

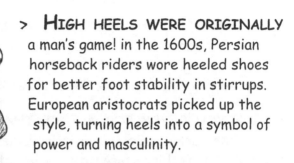

> **HIGH HEELS WERE ORIGINALLY** a man's game! in the 1600s, Persian horseback riders wore heeled shoes for better foot stability in stirrups. European aristocrats picked up the style, turning heels into a symbol of power and masculinity.

> **GET READY FOR** a sizzling story! in 1946, French engineer Louis Réard designed the scandalous modern bikini, exposing the navel for the first time. Named after the atomic bomb testing site, Bikini Atoll, Réard hoped his creation would have an explosive impact on fashion. And indeed, it did! in Italy, a young woman received a ticket for wearing a bikini in public, making headlines worldwide. Fast forward to today, bikinis are a beachwear staple, but back then, they caused quite a stir!

> **THE INGENIOUS INUIT PEOPLE CRAFTED** "Eskimo sunglasses" from bone, ivory, or wood, featuring narrow slits to reduce snow glare. One day, an inuit hunter, tired of squinting against the icy reflections, carved a pair for himself and revolutionized Arctic eyewear! These nifty goggles not only protected their eyes from the sun's blinding rays but also set the stage for today's snow goggles. Talk about an ice-solated fashion statement!

> **MAKE WAY FOR THE "S-BEND" CORSET!** Popular in the early 1900s, this bizarre fashion contraption forced women into an unnatural posture, thrusting the chest forward and the hips back. Thankfully, more comfortable undergarments eventually replaced this posture hazard.

> IT'S HARD TO FATHOM, BUT DURING THE Victorian era, arsenic was used to create a vibrant green dye for clothing. Sadly, the toxic fabric caused numerous deaths, earning the nickname "killer green."

> ARE YOU READY FOR A FACT THAT'LL BUG YOU out? in the early 1900s, trendsetting ladies in Mexico flaunted their fashion sense with live insects! That's right—instead of diamonds and pearls, they opted for the Maquech beetle, glammed up with precious stones. These living baubles were pinned onto their clothing, crawling about as a bizarre but fabulous brooch. Can you imagine the buzz these critter couture pieces created in high society? Now that's a fashion statement with legs!

> EVER WONDERED WHY PIRATES ALWAYS seemed to have an eye patch? It wasn't because they were all losing eyes in swashbuckling fights. The real reason is surprisingly practical! Pirates wore eye patches to keep one eye adapted to night vision. This way, when they moved below deck from the bright sunlight, they could simply switch the patch to the other eye and see in the dark immediately!

THINGS
HISTORICAL FIGURES DID

> HOLD ONTO YOUR STOVEPIPE HATS! ABRAHAM Lincoln, one of America's most revered presidents, was also an accomplished wrestler in his younger years. With over 300 matches under his belt, Honest Abe only lost once. Who knew the Great Emancipator had such mad grappling skills?

> **DID YOU KNOW THAT NAPOLEON BONAPARTE**
wasn't actually short? The French emperor stood at 5'7 ",
which was quite average for his time. The myth of his
short stature likely stemmed from British propaganda and
the nickname "le petit caporal," which was affectionate
rather than a comment on his height. Turns out, his "short
man complex" was just a tall tale!

> **PROLIFIC ARTIST VINCENT**
van Gogh wasn't just famous for his
post-impressionist masterpieces.
In a fit of madness, he once cut off
part of his own ear! This event occurred
in December 1888 during a tumultuous
period of van Gogh's life marked by
mental instability and severe emotional
distress. Shortly after the incident,
he painted the famous "Self-Portrait
with Bandaged Ear". Talk about
suffering for your art.

> **CHARLIE CHAPLIN, THE KING OF SILENT**
comedy, once entered a Charlie Chaplin look-alike contest...
and lost! The judges clearly missed the memo on who the
real deal was. What a slapstick twist of fate!

> **THE INFAMOUS CLEOPATRA, QUEEN OF ANCIENT**
Egypt, wasn't actually Egyptian! She was of Greek descent
and was the first of her dynasty to speak the Egyptian
language. Talk about shaking up the royal bloodline!

> **LEONARDO DA VINCI, THE ULTIMATE**
Renaissance man, loved napping... but with a twist! He did
this polyphasic sleep thing, taking 15-minute naps every
four hours, which added up to only 1.5 hours of sleep a day.
No wonder he had time for all those amazing inventions!

> **ALBERT EINSTEIN, THE GENIUS PHYSICIST,** had a quirky sense of style that people didn't always notice. He didn't like socks, thinking they were too constricting. He thought going sockless made him feel free and relaxed. Later in life, he wore the same gray suit every day, believing it saved time and made his life simpler. It's like Einstein's personal theory of fashion relativity, showing that even brilliant minds can be a bit eccentric when it comes to dressing up!

> **PICTURE THIS: TRYING TO GIVE YOUR HOLIDAY** dinner a little zap of electricity! That's what Benjamin Franklin, the ever-curious scientist, tried to do in December 1750. Fascinated by electricity, he thought electrocuting a turkey would make it more tender. Unfortunately, things went wrong, and he zapped himself instead! Not only did this shocking experience give him a whole new respect for electricity, it left him sore for a couple of days

> **JULIUS CAESAR, THE ICONIC ROMAN GENERAL** and statesman, got into a bit of a jam in 75 BC when pirates kidnapped him. Unfazed by the situation, he brazenly told his captors that their ransom demand was embarrassingly low for a man of his stature. Once the ransom was paid and he was freed, Caesar organizing a fleet to hunt down the pirates and ultimately had them crucified as a testament to his unshakable resolve. Talk about a plan that really backfired!

> **THE INTREPID MARCO POLO WASN'T JUST AN** explorer—he was also a bit of a fibber! in his travel accounts, he claimed to have been the governor of a Chinese city, but historians have found no evidence to support his tall tale. Looks like Marco's pants were on fire!

INCREDIBLE FACTS FOR INQUISITIVE MINDS

THE GREATEST EXPLORERS & THEIR DISCOVERIES

> **HERE'S A HOT TAKE: FERDINAND MAGELLAN,** the first person to circumnavigate the globe, didn't actually complete the journey himself! He was killed in the Philippines, and his remaining crew continued the voyage without him. So close, yet so far!

> **CAPTAIN JAMES COOK, THE BOLD BRITISH** explorer, must have gotten the surprise of his life when he bumped into Australia in 1770! His original mission? To observe the transit of Venus across the sun. Instead, he ended up saying 'G'day mate!' to a whole new continent! That's like heading out to mow the lawn and finding a hidden treasure chest!

> **ZHENG HE, THE CHINESE ADMIRAL,** commanded a fleet so enormous that it would have made Columbus's ships look like toy boats! His massive treasure ships carried precious goods and exotic animals, making him the envy of every explorer on the high seas.

> **SIR ERNEST SHACKLETON, THE ANTARCTIC** explorer, had the ultimate "never give up" attitude. When his ship, the endurance, became trapped in ice, he and his crew survived for 20 months before being rescued. Now that's what we call an ice-cold determination!

> **THINK CLIMBING MOUNT EVEREST IS TOUGH?** Try doing it in a tweed suit! Sir George Mallory, a true fashion-forward adventurer, scaled the world's tallest peak back in the 1920s sporting his trusty tweed. Talk about a dapper daredevil!

> **AMERIGO VESPUCCI,** a pickle dealer turned explorer from bustling Florence, Italy, certainly left his mark in the 15th century. Not one, but two continents are named after him - North and South America. Just imagine, from selling pickles to having continents named after you. Talk about a career pivot!

> **IF YOU THOUGHT COLUMBUS'** fleet was impressive, wait till you hear about Zheng He. This Chinese explorer from the early Ming Dynasty in the 15th century commanded a fleet that would dwarf Columbus' into tiny rubber ducks. His treasure ships were reportedly so gigantic, you could fit four standard European ships in the cargo hold alone!

> **REWIND TO THE 18TH CENTURY, WHERE** French woman Jeanne Baret broke all norms. Disguising herself as a man, she became the first woman to circumnavigate the globe. Her daring exploits started in 1766, from her native France, and involved many close calls, including a violent mutiny. Clearly, Baret was not one to shy away from a challenge!

> **HERE'S A LITTLE TALE ABOUT FERDINAND** Magellan, a daredevil Portuguese sailor from Sabrosa. In 1519, this fellow decided to do a victory lap but not around a sports field, oh no, around the entire globe! Magellan and his crew sailed roughly 60,000 miles – now that's a lot of sea shanties!. So, next time you plan a road trip, remember - Magellan probably has you beat!

> **FASTEN YOUR OXYGEN MASKS FOR THIS ONE!**
in 1953, Sir Edmund Hillary, a New Zealander, and Tenzing Norgay, a Sherpa of Nepal, became the first to conquer Mount Everest. Their only reward at the 29,031 feet summit? An awe-inspiring view and the knowledge of a job well done.

> **CAN YOU IMAGINE LEAVING HOME FOR**
a fishing trip and accidentally discovering a whole new land? That's exactly what happened to Leif Erikson, a Norse explorer from Iceland, around the year 1000. Leif and his crew were swept off course and ended up in what is now believed to be Newfoundland, Canada, making him likely the first European to set foot in North America, 500 years before Columbus! Talk about a fishing tale for the ages!

> **NOW, LET'S MOVE ON TO A STORY OF**
determination and courage. Ernest Shackleton, an Irish-born British explorer, led an expedition to Antarctica in 1915, hoping to cross the continent. Unfortunately, his ship got trapped in ice. Not one to give up easily, Shackleton and his crew lived on the ice for over a year before they could be rescued. And you thought being stuck in traffic was bad!

STRANGE TRADITIONS FROM ANCIENT CIVILIZATIONS

> **GET READY FOR A BUMPY RIDE! THE ANCIENT**
Mayans believed that the world was carried on the back of a giant cosmic crocodile. This scaly critter swam through the sky, making sure the Earth stayed afloat. Crikey!

> **CAT LOVERS UNITE! THE ANCIENT EGYPTIANS**
didn't just adore their kitties; they practically worshiped
them. Picture this: 525 BC, the Battle of Pelusium, where
the cunning Persians used cats as shields, leading to an
Egyptian forfeit. They literally chose to lose a battle
rather than harm a hair on those precious kitty heads.
Now that's what I call a purr-suasive strategy!

> **EVER THINK YOUR VOTE DOESN'T COUNT?**
Try being an Ancient Greek! They'd scribble the name
of the most annoying Athenian on a shard of pottery,
an ostrakon, and bam! If you got enough votes, you were
exiled for a decade. Pottery shard elections, folks.
Democracy with a ceramic twist!

> **LET'S SPIN THE GLOBE TO THE 16TH CENTURY**
Aztec Empire. Every year, they'd select a perfect youth to
live like royalty, only for the unlucky lad to be sacrificed
to the gods after a year. That's the kind of promotion
you'd probably want to pass on!

> **LET'S TAKE A WALK ON THE WILD SIDE WITH**
the Spartan boys. They had an annual event called
'diamastigosis,' where they'd whip each other in a display of
machismo. Nothing says brotherhood like a good ol' whip-off!

> **OVER IN THE MAYAN CIVILIZATION, THEY TOOK**
beauty standards to new heights...or should I say lengths?
They'd squish infants' foreheads with boards to elongate their
skulls, a practice known as "Artificial Cranial Deformation".
A heady mix of beauty and brawn, if you ask me!

> **PICTURE THIS: VICTORIAN-ERA FAMILY PHOTO,**
everyone's dressed to the nines, smiling...including dear
Uncle Bob who passed away last week. Yes, friends,
post-mortem photography was all the rage. Say "cheese,"!

> **THE HEIAN PERIOD IN JAPAN** introduced a gothic fashion trend centuries ahead of its time: black teeth. Aristocrats would regularly dye their teeth using a mixture called Ohaguro. Trendsetting or terrifying? You decide!

> **THE MAORI PEOPLE OF NEW** Zealand have a greeting that could give the French a run for their money. It's called the hongi, where they press noses together. Beats the awkward cheek-kiss tango, doesn't it?

> **THE ANCIENT EGYPTIAN PHARAOHS WERE** the original trendsetters of the hat game. They never let anyone see their hair, always donning headdresses called nemes. A perpetual bad hair day, or just fashion-forward? We may never know!

> **THROWING RICE AT WEDDINGS? TOO** mainstream for the Middle Ages Europeans! They tossed shoes at newlyweds for good luck. That's one way to kickstart a marriage!

THE RISE & FALL OF THE WORLD'S EMPIRES

> **LET'S START OFF WITH THE ROMAN EMPIRE,** which was bossing the world around from 27 BC to 476 AD. From North Africa's sandy beaches to Scotland's misty highlands, they had their Roman fingers in many pies.

They ruled longer than the United States has been a country! Their secret? A solid legal system and a flair for dramatic gladiator fights. But alas! When barbarians came knocking in 476 AD, the party was over. Talk about an uninvited party pooper!

> **NOW, WE WHOOSH OVER TO THE** steppes of Asia, the playground of the Mongol Empire from 1206 to 1368. Under Genghis Khan, a shepherd boy turned conqueror, they built the largest land empire in history. Their postal system, the Yam, was so speedy that by the time you said "express delivery," your package was at the door! But power struggles and rebellions eventually split them up. Guess, too much of a good thing...

> **NEXT, WE'RE OFF TO THE LAND OF THE** Pharaohs, Ancient Egypt, strutting its stuff from 3100 BC to 30 BC. These trendsetters were into mummification, pyramid building, and cat-worship before it was cool. When Cleopatra, the last Pharaoh, cozied up with Rome, the kingdom said its final goodbyes. Even pyramids couldn't cushion that fall!

> **SWINGING BY THE PERSIAN EMPIRE NOW,** we find Cyrus and Darius the Great ruling over an empire stretching from Greece to india from 550 BC to 330 BC. They respected diversity, built highways before highways were a thing, and they reigned longer than most Hollywood

marriages! But when Alexander the Great took a little detour to Persia, it was checkmate. I'm sure they wish he missed the turnoff!

> **QUICK! GRAB YOUR SUNHAT! WE'RE ZOOMING** to the Aztec Empire in Mexico. From 1345 to 1521, they transformed marshy land into a metropolis, Tenochtitlan, that would put modern city planners to shame. But when Spanish conquistadors arrived with shiny beads and nasty germs, the empire crumbled like a stale taco.

> **LET'S WALTZ OVER TO THE LUXURIOUS** Ottoman Empire, lounging across three continents from 1299 to 1922. These folks were the tastemakers of their time, with grand bazaars and monumental architecture. But when nationalism began to simmer in the 19th century, it was time to say "hoşça kal" (that's goodbye in Turkish) to the empire.

> **THE BRITISH EMPIRE, WHERE THE SUN** apparently forgot to set from the 16th century to the mid-20th century. These champs were really into exploration, tea-drinking, and playing 'musical chairs' with countries. But two World Wars and a pinch of decolonization and a sprinkle of democracy later, the sun had finally set on the Queens Empire.

> **LETS POP OVER TO THE HAN DYNASTY** in China, ruling from 206 BC to 220 AD. They brought us paper, the Silk Road, and the Great Wall, which is still standing today – talk about solid construction! But when a series of revolts broke out, the dynasty crumbled faster than a fortune cookie.

> **LET'S TALK ABOUT THE MAURYAN EMPIRE**
in india. They ruled from 322 BC to 187 BC. Their big boss,
Emperor Ashoka, changed his mind after an epic battle
left him worn. He decided to follow Buddhism, and told
everyone about it. Soon thereafter, the empire fell apart
quicker than a sandcastle at high tide! Was it due to his
newfound peaceful nature? We can only guess!

> **NOW, LET'S HEAD TO WEST**
Africa, where the Mali Empire was
super rich from the 13th to the
16th centuries. Their leader,
Mansa Musa, had so much gold
that even the richest people
today might feel a little
jealous! This empire helped
make Islamic and African
art really cool. But, like
a game of musical chairs
that got out of hand,
the empire fell apart
because of family fights
and invasions.

> **ALRIGHTY, LET'S JET OVER TO SOUTH**
America, where the inca Empire was hanging out
from 1438 to 1533. These guys were all about that
mountain life, building incredible cities like Machu Picchu
right up in the Andes! They also made the first highways
in the Americas – long before Route 66 was a twinkle
in anyone's eye. But then the Spanish conquistadors rocked
up, and the inca Empire went down quicker than a phone
battery on 1%.

INCREDIBLE FACTS FOR INQUISITIVE MINDS

> **NOW, WE'RE ZOOMING OFF TO EASTERN**
Europe, where the Byzantine Empire was kicking it from
330 AD to 1453 AD. They were masters of the arts
and education, kind of like the cool, cultured cousin you
always look up to. They gave us some truly mind-blowing
mosaics and domed buildings. But the party stopped
when the Ottoman Turks came a-knocking. Talk about
a major buzzkill!

> **LET'S TAKE A STROLL OVER TO THE ARABIAN**
Peninsula where the Abbasid Caliphate was in charge from
750 AD to 1258 AD. They were like the cool nerds of
their day, loving science, math, and philosophy. They gave
us algebra and hospitals! But when the Mongols showed up
in 1258, it was game over.

> **WE'RE HEADING DOWN UNDER TO THE**
legendary Aboriginal cultures of Australia. These guys
have been around for over 60,000 years! They taught
us about the Dreamtime and gave us the boomerang.
But, when the British arrived in 1788, they experience
quite the change in vibes!

> **NOW, LET'S FLY BACK TO THE**
Mediterranean, where Alexander
the Great was ruling the roost
from 336 BC to 323 BC. This
fella was a real conqueror,
grabbing lands from Greece all
the way to Egypt and india. He
was so good at making friends
and influencing people, they called
it the Hellenistic period, a real
cultural mash-up of Greek and

Eastern styles. But, like the battery on your phone after a day of non-stop social media, Alexander's empire ran out of juice quickly after his death. The big dogs of his empire bickered and argued until it all fell apart. Talk about not being able to play nice!

> **NEXT, WE'RE OFF TO THE** snowy lands of Russia, where the Tsardom of Russia ruled the roost from 1547 to 1721. These folks were tough cookies, dealing with long winters and big furry bears. They built the iconic St. Basil's Cathedral and established the Russian Orthodox Church. But, like the final plot twist in a movie, Peter the Great shook things up, turned the Tsardom into an Empire and moved the capital from Moscow to his new city, Saint Petersburg. Whoa, talk about a major makeover!

> **LET'S NOW SCOOT OVER TO THE ISLAND** nation of Japan, where the Samurais of Tokugawa Shogunate where holding the fort from 1603 to 1868. Although fierce, these guys were all about order and peace, kinda like the hall monitor at school. They gave us haiku poetry and some epic teas. But when Commodore Perry from the US rolled up with his 'Black Ships', it was like the school bully arriving at the peaceful playground. The Shogunate crumbled, and the Emperor was back in charge.

INCREDIBLE FACTS FOR INQUISITIVE MINDS

> LASTLY, WE'RE LANDING IN THE INDIAN
subcontinent, where the Mughal Empire flourished from
1526 to 1857. These guys were big on architecture,
giving us the beautiful Taj Mahal and a love for biryani!
But when the British East india Company started to
take control, it was like your friend suddenly beating
you at your own game. The last Mughal Emperor,
Bahadur Shah II, was exiled and the Empire was history.
What a bummer, right?

CONCLUSION

WELL, MY FRIENDS, WE'VE REACHED THE END of our knowledge-packed journey together, and what an exhilarating adventure it's been! We've uncovered the hidden truths of the universe - all the way from the smallest critters on Earth, to the mysteries outer space and beyond!

incredible Facts for inquisitive Minds has been your trusty guide on this trivia-packed trip, unlocking the doors of peculiar knowledge on every page.

And while we've reached the end of this book, remember that the journey of learning never ends. With every new day, there's always something fresh to discover, another fact to ponder, and another question to ask.

So, take a bow, brave explorers! You've soaked up over 1000 mind-boggling facts about science, history, pop culture, and the weird world we live in!

But don't stop here. Continue to satiate your curiosity, keep asking questions, and remember, every conversation, every book, and every question can be a portal to a world of new and interesting knowledge.

Thank you for joining us on this wild ride of discovery, we hope you enjoyed it as much as we did.

So, until next time, keep that inquisitive spirit alive, stay curious, and always be ready to learn something new.

Remember, in this vast and incredible universe, there's always something fascinating to uncover!

Made in the USA
Middletown, DE
14 May 2024

54316447R00110